The Hidden History of Zionism

The Hidden History of Zionism

By Ralph Schoenman

Veritas Press
Santa Barbara, Calif.

The Hidden History of Zionism
By Ralph Schoenman
Copyright © 1988 by Ralph Schoenman
All rights reserved

Library of Congress Catalog Card Number: 88–50585

ISBN: 0–929675–00–2   (Hardcover)
ISBN: 0–929675–01–0   (Paperback)

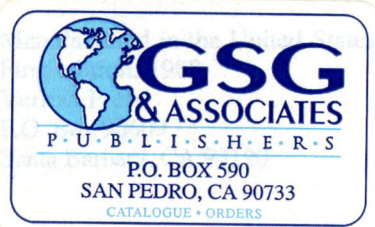

Cover designed by Mya Shone
Cover photograph by Donald McCullin
(As printed in *The Palestinians* by Jonathan Dimbleby, Quartet Books, Ltd.)

To The Memory of Khalid Ahmed Zaki
Fallen Comrade and Beloved Friend

* * *

For Hamdi Faraj and Mohammed Manasrah
"Thawra Hatta al Nas'r"

Acknowledgements

During the Dark Ages in Europe, Greek science, mathematics and philosophy were preserved by Arab scholars. From Avicenna to al-Kindi, Arab science and mathematics nurtured the legacy of Greek natural and moral philosophy.

The Zionist movement subdued Palestine and assaulted its culture with a relentless barbarity shocking even to those familiar with the cruel annals of colonial conquest. This history has been suppressed during the past one hundred years. It has only been brought to light through the writings of a relatively few intrepid scholars.

A profound debt is owed to them—Moslems, Christians, Jews and non-believers—whose work of preservation and exegesis has made possible this attempt at synthesis.

Alan Benjamin has devoted hundreds of hours to all facets of this work. Co-thinker, discussant, editor and friend, he has sharpened the analysis, economized the presentation and taken charge of multiple technical problems inherent in its production. It would not exist without him.

Mya Shone, my wife and companion, but for her own reticence would be listed as the co-author of this book. Her role in writing and shaping the text is equal to my own. Every sentence has been tested by her insistence on precision of expression and lucidity. To the extent that either has been achieved, the energy and will flowed from her, the writing shared in a labor of love.

To our treasured Palestinian friends and comrades, I would paraphrase Dylan Thomas: We are alone and not alone in the unknown world, our bliss and suffering forever shared and forever all our own.

Contents

	Preface: The Uprising	1
1.	The Four Myths	15
2.	Zionist Objectives	17
3.	Colonizing Palestine	27
4.	Tragic Consequences	31
5.	The Seizure of the Land	41
6.	Zionism and the Jews	47
7.	The Myth of Security	59
8.	Blitzkrieg and Slaughter	63
9.	The Second Occupation	71
10.	The Prevalence of Torture	77
11.	The Prisons	95
12.	Strategy for Conquest	103
13.	A Strategy for Revolution	121
	Map: The Zionist Vision of "Eretz Israel"	134
	Footnotes	135
	Suggested Reading	141
	Appendix	143
	About the Author	150

PREFACE

The Uprising

"With anger, hatred, and sheer ferocity, thousands of youngsters hurled rocks at their Israeli occupiers, undaunted by the gunfire that greeted them. This was more than civil unrest. ... It was the beginning of a civil rebellion."[1]

This is how *Jerusalem Post* correspondent Hirsh Goodman described the uprising of Palestinian youth in the West Bank and Gaza in mid-December 1987.

Goodman's remarks were written the day before the December 21, 1987, general strike which engulfed every Palestinian community under Israeli rule. The strike was described by the Israeli daily, *Ha'aretz,* as "writing on our wall even more serious than the bloody riots of the last two weeks."[2]

"On that day," wrote John Kifner in *The New York Times*, "the vast army of Arab laborers who wait on tables, pick vegetables, haul garbage, lay brick and perform virtually all Israel's menial work, stayed home."[3]

The Israeli response to the uprising was brutal. Defense Minister Yitzhak Rabin ordered the use of tanks, armored vehicles and automatic rifles against an unarmed population.

The *San Francisco Examiner* cited Rabin as openly advocating assassination. "They can shoot to hit leaders of disorder," Rabin said in defense of the army's practice of using marksmen with high-powered .22-caliber rifles to shoot indiscriminately at Palestinian youth.[4]

Rabin ordered house-to-house searches, first for young men and later for anyone of whom an example might be made. By December 27, over 2,500 Palestinians were seized, many of them as young as twelve; by the end of January the number reached 4,000 and was rising.[5] The "militants" were marked for deportation. Israeli high-security jails and detention centers were overflowing. Mass trials of Palestinians were underway.

The act of brutality which most inflamed the Palestinian population was the army seizure of the wounded from hospital beds. This practice, standard procedure throughout the invasion of Lebanon in 1982, made Shifa Hospital in Gaza a center of resistance. Great crowds amassed to defend the wounded, whom, they rightfully feared, would never be seen again.

"The youngsters in Gaza and the West Bank where riots erupted," wrote *Jerusalem Post* correspondent Hirsh Goodman "have not received any terrorist training, nor are they members of a terrorist organization. Rather they are members of that Palestinian generation that grew up knowing nothing but occupation."[6]

A mother of a Palestinian man shot three times in the head by Israeli soldiers was asked if she would let her remaining sons join the demonstrations. "As long as I am alive," she responded, "I am going to teach the young people to fight. ... I don't care whatever happens, as long as we get our land."[7]

Rashad Shawa'a, deposed Mayor of Gaza, expressed the same sentiment:

"The youth have lost hope that Israel will ever give them their rights. They feel the Arab countries are unable to accomplish anything. They feel that the Palestine Liberation Organization (P.L.O.) has failed to achieve a thing."[8]

Los Angeles Times correspondent Dan Fisher's account is even more significant:

"This new-found sense of unity has been one of the most striking changes to foreign observers and non-Gaza Palestinians. ... It is a phenomenon that extends to previous divisions between young and old and between those who work in Israel and those who do not."[9]

Force, Might, Beatings

As the uprising intensified, the Israeli cabinet and Defense Minister Yitzhak Rabin implemented "collective punishment," a tactic characteristic of the Nazi occupation of France, Denmark and Yugoslavia. Food, water and medicine were prevented from reaching Palestinian refugee camps in Gaza and the West Bank. The United Nations Relief and Works Agency for Palestine Refugees in the Near East (U.N.R.W.A.) personnel reported that children seeking powdered milk at U.N. depots were shot at and beaten with sticks.

The Casbah, where over half of the 125,000 inhabitants of Nablus live, has been sealed off by concrete barricades and iron gates. Qabatiya and the nearby refugee camp at Jenin were placed under siege. At the time of writing, the siege, which has cut off all food, water, fuel and electricity, has lasted fifty-five days.

A *Jerusalem Post* analyst explained the policies of Rabin:

"The first priority is to use force, might, beatings. [This] is considered more effective than detention ... [because] he may then resume stoning soldiers. But if troops break his hand, he won't be able to throw stones...."[10]

By the next day, the news media were reporting the most bestial beatings by soldiers throughout the West Bank and Gaza. The account by John Kifner was compelling:

"NABLUS, Israeli Occupied West Bank, January 22: Both hands encased in plaster casts, Imad Omar Abu Rub explained from his bed in the Rafidiya Hospital what happened when the Israeli Army came to the Palestinian village of Qabatiya.

"'They entered the house like animals, shouting,' the 22-year old student at Bir Zeit University said. 'They took us from the house, kicking us in the head, beating us, all the soldiers with their rifle butts.'

"Then he was taken to the construction site of an unfinished house where, he said, the soldiers put an empty bucket over his head.

"Several of the soldiers held him down, he said, gripping his arms to force his hands against a rock. Two others, he said, beat his hands with lengths of two-by-fours, breaking the bones.

"The injuries are the product of a new officially declared policy of the Israeli Army and the police to beat up Palestinians in hopes of ending the wave of protests in the occupied West Bank and Gaza Strip that began in early December. At least thirty-eight Palestinians have been killed by Israeli gunfire in the protests.

"In the bed next to Mr. Abu Rub's, Hassan Arif Kemal, a 17-year-old high school student from Qabatiya, told a nearly identical story."[11]

Labor and Likud leaders responded with one voice to world-wide outcry over these practices. President Chaim Herzog declared: "The alternative facing us today ... is between suppressing these riots or allowing them to develop into a new Teheran or Beirut."[12]

John Kifner reported in *The New York Times:*

"Prime Minister Yitzhak Shamir and Defense Minister Yitzhak Rabin continued to defend the policy, with both men saying publicly that the purpose of the beatings was to instill fear of the Israeli army in Palestinians."

Shamir stated that events had "shattered the barrier of fear. ... Our task is to recreate that barrier and once again put the fear of death into the Arabs of the areas...."

He concluded that the uprising would never have taken place "had the troops used firearms from the very first moment."[13]

Palestinian Resistance Grows

The rebellion of the Palestinian people of the West Bank and Gaza has engulfed every village, town and refugee camp. Children as young as eight and old people in their seventies and eighties defy the Israeli army daily. Entire village populations, waving makeshift Palestinian flags of bedsheets and cloth, mass defiantly, singing and chanting and hurling stones at soldiers firing automatic weapons.

The Great Uprising—the "Intifadeh"—has become a symbol of Palestinian nationhood as the brutal repression that once filled the people with despair now fuels their determination and will, which encompasses the readiness to die.

The Israeli reprisals have been barbarous. The repression has been unleashed with particular savagery against the refugee camps and the old quarters of the cities inhabited by the impoverished.

By April 1988 over 150 Palestinians had died. The Israeli government had admitted to the arrest of 2,000 people, bringing the acknowledged total to 4,000. The real figure was far higher.

Sources in the West Bank and Gaza established that the number detained by the weekend of March 27 had exceeded 13,000. Bassam Shaka'a, deposed Mayor of Nablus, placed the total held solely in a hastily constructed barbed-wire encampment at Dhariyah at 10,000.

In the Balata camp outside Nablus, and in the Casbah—the old quarter—1,000 people were arrested in a period of 48 hours. The discovery of people in ditches in the fields—shot in the back or with their heads caved in—has been reported from villages throughout the West Bank and Gaza.

Bassam Shaka'a described the rampage of the Israeli armed units:

"No matter which house one calls, the anguished accounts of family members wounded or arrested pour forth. Convoys of buses cruise the streets of Nablus followed by vans of the Mossad, Israel's secret police. Army units go from house to house pulling youths from their beds at 3 a.m. As the buses fill, the soldiers beat the youths viciously around the head, shins, groin and back. Shrieks fill the air.

"As the army makes its rounds kidnapping the young from their homes, people gather at their windows and on the roofs of houses shouting in unison, 'Falistin Arabia, Thawra Hatta al Nas'r, Allah

Akhbar'" [Arab Palestine, Revolution Until Victory, God is Great].13a

Bassam Shaka'a described the attempts by the Israeli army to spread panic and terror in Nablus and outlying villages:

"Fleets of helicopters fly over Nablus at night dropping a dense, green toxic gas over the city. The smell pervades every house. Armed units fire canisters of the substance into houses at random. Doctors at Ittihad Hospital reported several deaths and severe lung injuries from this as-yet unidentified asphyxiating chemical, totally distinct from tear gas."

Among the victims were the grandmother of the Da'as family and the 100-year-old father of noted Nablus attorney Mohammad Irshaid. Soldiers had entered the house at 2 a.m., smashing furniture and firing a canister of the dreaded green gas while preventing the family from leaving.

Two of the children, ages 9 and 11, were taken by the soldiers in their night clothes, frog-marched in the streets and beaten as they were forced by the jeering soldiers to clear debris.

Simultaneously, the Israeli army targeted the hospitals. Army trucks rammed ambulances and blocked them from reaching the homes of those overcome by the gas. Soldiers entered the Ittihad Hospital in Nablus numerous times, arresting the wounded and those waiting to give blood to family members. Even the operating theater was invaded while surgeons were operating on patients.

Doctors were beaten and equipment smashed. Family members were prevented from entering the hospital and the cars of doctors and nurses were destroyed by soldiers.

Meanwhile, all of Nablus was paralyzed by a total strike. All the streets in every quarter of the city were without open shops or business activity. As gas permeated the city, cries and chants filled the night.

Gas canisters recovered by Bassam Shaka'a, Yousef al-Masri [chief of Ittihad Hospital] and American author Alfred Lilienthal bear the markings "560 cs. Federal Lab. Saltsburg, Pa. USA MK2 1988." Biochemists are studying their properties as casualties mount.

John Kifner reported on April 4 that "Hundreds of refugees were treated in United Nations clinics for gas inhalation." On April 15, Kifner wrote, "...gas has been thrown inside homes, clinics and schools where the effects are particularly severe."13b

His report was the first, after four months of the use of such chemical weapons, to acknowledge the fact:

"Agency doctors have seen symptoms not normally connected with tear gas, and U.N.R.W.A. is seeking information on the contents of the gas ... to provide antidote ... especially for the most vulnerable groups ... pregnant women, the very young and elderly."

Kifner later reported, "Warnings on the canisters say the contents can be lethal." Throughout the West Bank and Gaza, cases of miscarriages, vaginal bleeding and asphyxiation were occurring after the use of the gas.

A Glimpse of the Savagery

One of the most vicious incidents occurred in the town of Qalqiya. Soldiers entered the house of workers and poured gasoline over them, setting them alight. Six workers were covered in flames. Four of the victims managed to rush out of the building and rolled on the ground, ripping off their clothes. Two were severely burned and are in critical condition.

On February 20, two youths were arrested in Khan Yunis, beaten savagely and taken to the beach where they were buried alive under the sand. After the soldiers left, villagers managed to dig them out.

Reports in the establishment press give a glimpse of the scale of Israeli brutality. A soldier's account reported in the Israeli newspaper Hadashot was cited in *Newsweek*:

"We got orders to knock on every door, enter and take out all the males. The younger ones we lined up with their faces against the wall, and soldiers beat them with billy-clubs. This was no private initiative. These were the orders from our company commander."[13c]

The accounts make clear that Israeli protestations about excesses of individual soldiers are transparently false. *Newsweek* revealed:

"Armed with 30-inch wooden clubs and urged by their prime minister to 'put the fear back into the Arabs,' Israeli soldiers have methodically beaten up Palestinians since early January, deliberately breaking bones and beating prisoners into unconsciousness. Casualties included not only young men ... but also women. Most of the injured shunned hospitals for fear of arrest."

The avoidance of hospitals by the injured has prevented accurate reporting of the vast scale of the savage beatings and of the deaths of those who endured them. But an indication was provided in the reports of the medical team inspecting the wounded in the hospitals in early

February 1988.

Dr. Jennifer Leaning, a faculty member of Harvard Medical School and a trauma specialist, reported her findings:

"There is a systematic pattern of limb injury that is clearly organized to cause fractures ... a consistent pattern of bonebreaks across the back of the hand and in the middle of the forearm that ... come from holding the hand or arm in place and applying a strong blow to the bone."[13d]

Dr. Leaning and the team of Physicians for Human Rights traveled throughout the West Bank and Gaza. They concluded, "It is a pattern that is controlled. A systematic pattern over a wide geographical area. It is as if they have been instructed."

Dr. Leaning's account of the new patients brought to Shifa Hospital in Gaza is compelling:

"They looked like they had been mauled. What is impressive is the number of fractures per patient. These patients look as if they had been put through a washing-machine wringer. They would have had to hold them down and just keep beating them."

Repeated instances of young males shot deliberately through the testicles were reported in Shifa Hospital in Gaza and Makassad Hospital in East Jerusalem. Soldiers poured boiling water over a 2-year-old infant, rendering her catatonic.

"Quelling the Protests"

New York Times correspondent John Kifner called the systematic roundups "part of a series of tough new measures, including economic sanctions and collective punishment, that the Israeli army and other officials are imposing in hopes of quelling the protests, which have grown into an increasingly organized Palestinian mass movement in the occupied West Bank and Gaza Strip."[13e]

The army's new orders allow detention without any specific charge or trials, even in military courts. Moveover, according to the March 23 *New York Times*, "the new procedures do away with judicial review of the administrative detention sentences and allow local commanders to order the arrests."

Immediately after the order, people were seized overnight in more than a dozen refugee districts, villages and towns in the West Bank and Gaza.

Israeli Defense Minister Yitzhak Rabin announced that Israeli civilians have the same authority as soldiers to shoot. He added that soldiers need not fire warning shots before shooting Palestinians.[13f]

Newsweek was more explicit: "The decree meant Israeli soldiers could shoot to kill Palestinian youths. ... Yitzhak Rabin [was] effectively deputizing settlers."[13g]

The decision, according to *Newsweek,* would "open the floodgates of the 60,000 settlers' pent-up frustration [sic]."

It was not long before an attack occurred. On April 6, settlers engaging in a clear provocation shot in cold blood a Palestinian working in his field outside the village of Beita. Attention, however, focused on the death of Tirza Porat, a 15-year-old settler girl among the group. The settlers reported Tirza Porat had been stoned to death by the Palestinian villagers, but an army autopsy report revealed she had been shot in the head by the Kahane follower acting as her nominal guard. [Rabbi Meir Kahane is the founder of the Jewish Defense League.]

Despite the autopsy report, Prime Minister Yitzhak Shamir used the occasion to vow that Palestinians "would be crushed like grasshoppers ... heads smashed against the boulders and walls."[13h]

In Beita village, the scene of the incident, thirty houses were blown up. The number of houses destroyed was confirmed by Hamdi Faraj, a noted Palestinian journalist.

Forms of Self-Government Emerge

The recent Palestinian uprising has done more to challenge Israeli control than had been achieved in twenty years. The entire infrastructure of Israeli rule has unraveled. Spies are asking forgiveness, confessing their deeds and exposing the apparatus of control. Police are resigning.

The Village Leagues, Israeli organizations of collaborators, have collapsed. The *Los Angeles Times* reports that challenges by the "Unified National Leadership of the Uprising" have led to resignations by municipal, village, and town councils.

Before the uprising, 20,000 Palestinians worked under Israeli army and police control, providing services to the West Bank and Gaza. They were teachers, clerks and administrators. Most have resigned.

Increasingly, forms of self-government are emerging in the West Bank and Gaza. The Israelis close the schools; the resistance organizes classes. The Israelis order shops to open; the resistance keeps them closed. The Israelis close the shops; the resistance opens them.

The West Bank and Gaza are trapped in what *Newsweek* calls a "colonial setup." *Newsweek* cites Israeli demographer Meron Benvenisti, the former Deputy Mayor of Jerusalem, as follows: "The Occupied Territories became a source of cheap labor and a captive market for Israeli goods."[13i]

Israel's trade surplus with the West Bank and Gaza, Benvenisti reveals, is $500 million a year. The government takes a further $80 million a year in taxes above what it provides in meager social services. The territories import $780 million a year of Israeli goods at high prices.

But the uprising has changed everything. *Newsweek* states:

"The Palestinians have some economic weapons of their own. Thousands of Arab workers had long since walked away from jobs at Israeli farms, factories and construction sites. Palestinian shoppers cut back their purchases of Israeli goods. Arab merchants and self-employed professionals struck a more direct blow at the occupation; they refused to pay Israeli income and commercial taxes."

Thus, as *Newsweek* acknowledges, the economic sword cut in two directions. Israel's construction industry which drew 42% of its workforce from the Occupied Territories "has been hobbled by Arab walkouts." Hotels in Jerusalem report a sharp drop in spring bookings.

Israeli Economic Minister Gad Yaacobi estimated that the first three months of "rioting" cost Israel's economy "at least $300 million"—10% of U.S. aid for a full year.

"Liberated Zones"

No respite can be expected for Israel. The villages in the West Bank and Gaza have responded defiantly to Israel's barbaric onslaught, declaring themselves "liberated zones," barricading their streets, and flying the Palestinian flag.

Newsweek reports: "Their protests are adroitly coordinated through leaflets issued by the shadowy Unified National Command of the Uprising. Their leaflets are the law of the land."[13j]

Despite the massive repression, Palestinian spirits have never been higher. This spirit is perhaps the factor of greatest concern to the Israeli state. Prime Minister Yitzhak Shamir told Israeli television:

"The people who are throwing stones, the inciters, the leaders, they are today in a situation of euphoria, of great enthusiasm. They think that they are the victors."

Middle East editor of the *Jerusalem Post* Yehudi Litani reported that "[Israeli] security forces estimate the army has now detained the majority of those now pulling the strings of the uprising"—and yet the uprising continues, the leaflets continue to appear, and a mood approaching panic is settling in among Israeli leaders.

On March 30, Land Day—the day Palestinians inside pre-1967 Israel protest the confiscation of their land—a general strike of Palestinians inside the pre-1967 borders was called. This action renewed a general strike in support of the uprising which was first held on December 21, 1987.

The Unified National Leadership of the Uprising in the Occupied Territories called for "huge demonstrations against the army and settlers" to coincide with the general strike.

For the first time since 1948, Palestinians throughout Lebanon—joined by Lebanese in Sidon, Beirut and other cities—also staged their own demonstrations and general strike in solidarity with the uprising.

The uprising has galvanized not only the Israeli Arabs, but the Palestinians in the Diaspora. The participation of the Palestinians of Lebanon and of thousands of Lebanese themselves was felt throughout the Arab world.

This new phase of the Palestinian revolution was not lost on the Israeli authorities. In an attempt to counter coordination between the Palestinians inside the "Green Line" [pre-1967 borders] and the Palestinians in the West Bank and Gaza, the Israelis completely "sealed off" the West Bank and Gaza.

"Since Intifadeh [Uprising] is taking place *both in the West Bank and in Israel*," [emphasis added] a senior military source said, "we decided to separate the two and to prevent large-scale public disorder."[13k]

"We want to signal very clearly that we are not going to hesitate to use whatever measures are necessary," Defense Minister Rabin said.

Ariel Sharon, former Defense Minister and current Trade Minister, announced that the uprising "would lead inevitably to war with the Arab states and the necessary expulsion of the Arabs from the West Bank, Gaza and the Galilee."[13l]

But the Palestinians, entering their 40th year of occupation since the founding of the Israeli state, have not been deterred. The "revolutionary war" of the Palestinian people is recruiting the hearts and minds of youth in every Arab country and in capitals across the world.

This spirit was fully captured in a letter written by members of the

Palestinian underground resistance in the Israeli-occupied West Bank to a rally in Paris, France, on March 3, 1988, organized by an ad-hoc committee of supporters of Palestinian human rights. Their letter states in part:

"Dear friends,

"We send you this letter from inside our beloved land—our land of honor, of dignity, courage and defiance—from our Palestine, from Jerusalem, the sacred city.

"We send you this letter in the name of our people, a patient people who are today standing tall and are waging a struggle unparalleled in our entire history.

"We want you to know that the Palestinian people have not been defeated. They are alive. They are struggling. They are saying that they will not accept humiliation and submission.

"The confidence of our people in the legitimacy of their struggle is immense. And our people know that their victory is certain— whatever the sacrifices, whatever the price that must be paid.

"Today, our people are suffering. They are shedding their blood to win their freedom, dignity, and honor; their right to determine their own destiny; their right to live in their homeland and to build a free, democratic, and sovereign state in all of Palestine.

"To all free men and women, to all our comrades, we say the following:

"The Palestinian people have been the victims for many decades of an international plot—of vicious attacks—aimed at exiling them and chasing them from the lands upon which they have lived for centuries.

"We have been expelled from our lands—lands which have now been settled by foreigners in accordance with the aims of colonialism and imperialism. This settlement has been imposed by the laws of oppression promoted by the Western nations and the Eastern totalitarian regimes. These oppressive laws are also those of international Zionism.

"We have been subject to terror, assassination and torture. Today, we are deprived of even our most elementary and legitimate rights.

"They have wanted to make of us an exiled people, destined permanently to refugee camps. They have wanted to destroy us physically and eliminate us.

"Through the wars of 1948 and 1967, they carried out the occupation of all of Palestine. But they forgot that by occupying all of Palestine they also unified the entire Palestinian people in their struggle against oppression.

"That is what is happening today as the children, the elderly, the women and the youth have risen up as one single person, without arms, to face the military machine of Zionism and imperialism—to face the violence of the guns, the clubs, the kidnappings, and the assassinations.

"Our weapons come from our homeland. They are the stones with which our people have built up a wall to defend their combatants and the Revolution.

"Dear friends: You should know what is going on in our homeland. Two weeks ago, the forces of occupation buried eight young Palestinians alive after having beaten them savagely and broken their limbs. Four of them were saved by the people; the other four were never found.

"Three days ago, Israeli military forces dropped three live Palestinian youths from a helicopter flying at a high altitude. One of the youths was only 13 years old.

"This is what they are currently doing to our people.

"Dear friends: We want you to know that we reject all so-called solutions and peace projects that some people would like to impose on us through international conferences. We want you to know that we are committed to continuing our revolution until the total liberation of all of Palestine, until the establishment of a democratic and free state in which all free men and women, from wherever they may be, are welcome to live so long as they accept to live with us as equals on our land of Palestine.

"We are no longer on our knees. We are standing tall. We will not yield. We feel that it is legitimate for us to demand aid and assistance from people throughout the world who are struggling for the freedom of all oppressed peoples.

"We ask of you not only that you speak out in support of our struggle in your speeches and protests but that you demand that your governments take a clear position in opposition to the repressive and criminal methods of Zionism. We ask for your moral and material support for our Palestinian people, who are struggling to obtain their final victory."

The Palestinian people have risen, their yearnings for emancipation stirring the pauperized masses in every country of the Arab East. Reduced to a condition of penury by corrupt, country-selling regimes, the Egyptian, Jordanian and Saudi people have begun to respond to the extraordinary example set for them by the Palestinian people.

Perhaps more significantly, a detailed report by Robert S. Greenberger in *The Wall Street Journal* describes the profound effect of the Intifadeh on the Jewish masses themselves, notably the Arab Jews, or Sephardim.

Now nearly 70% of the Jewish population of Israel, their sentiments are shifting. In contrast to rabid Likud [Israel's ruling party] figures such as Reuvin Rivlin, who declaimed ominously, "I believe God is Jewish. I believe the demographic problem will be solved," the Sephardic Jews are responding differently:

"The riots shattered the myth perpetuated by Likud founder Menachem Begin and his successor Prime Minister Yitzhak Shamir. ... The Sephardim are demanding social services and want to bridge the gap between ideology and practical solutions to the Arab-Israeli conflict. ... They care more about jobs, housing and education than keeping faith with a territorially inviolate Israel."[13m]

Henoch Smith, a U.S. pollster, reflecting on the new "challenge" from the Sephardim, notes: "This year, for the first time, they will account for 51% of voters."

As the letter from the underground attests, the Palestinian people, self-activated and increasingly confident of the power of mass struggle, are demanding "aid and assistance from people throughout the world who are struggling for the freedom of all oppressed peoples."

This message is beginning to reach Israeli Jews. The day is dawning when they too will seek a future free of a Zionist state which has combined subjugation of the Palestinian people with the exploitation of the Jewish poor.

This book seeks to uncover the hidden history of Zionism, a movement rooted in the ideology of racist oppression of Jews and colonial subjects alike. It has been written in anticipation of that day when the dedication and fervor of the Palestinian people, so long persecuted and oppressed, will speak to the Jews, recalling to them their own painful history, with a program for a Palestine in which victims, past and present, will create together the Intifadeh of the future and overthrow a state predicated upon oppression, torture, expulsion, expansion and unending war.

Ralph Schoenman,
Santa Barbara, Calif.
April 19, 1988

CHAPTER ONE

The Four Myths

It is not accidental that when anyone attempts to examine the nature of Zionism—its origins, history and dynamics—they meet with people who terrorize or threaten them. Quite recently, after mentioning a meeting on the plight of the Palestinian people during an interview on KPFK, a Los Angeles radio station, the organizers of the public meeting were deluged with bomb threats from anonymous callers.

Nor is it easy in the United States or Western Europe to disseminate information about the nature of Zionism or to analyze the specific events which denote Zionism as a political movement. Even the announcement on university campuses of authorized forums or meetings on the subject invariably engenders a campaign designed to close off discussion. Posters are torn down as fast as they are put up. Meetings are packed by flying squads of Zionist youth who seek to break them up. Literature tables are vandalized and leaflets and articles appear accusing the speaker of anti-Semitism or, in the case of those of Jewish origin, of self-hatred.

Vindictiveness and slander are so universally meted out to anti-Zionists because the disparity between the official fiction about Zionism and the Israeli state, on the one hand, and the barbarous practice of this colonial ideology and coercive apparatus, on the other, is so vast. People are in shock when they have an opportunity to hear or read about the century of persecution suffered by the Palestinians, and, thus, the apologists for Zionism are relentless in seeking to prevent coherent, dispassionate examination of the virulent and chauvinist record of the Zionist movement and of the state which embodies its values.

The irony of this is that when we study what the Zionists have written and said—particularly when addressing themselves—no doubt remains about what they have done or of their place in the political spectrum, dating from the last quarter of the 19th century to the present day.

Four overriding myths have shaped the consciousness of most people in our society about Zionism.

The **first** is that of "A land without a people for a people without a land." This myth was sedulously cultivated by early Zionists to promote the fiction that Palestine was a remote, desolate place ready for the taking. This claim was quickly followed by denial of Palestinian identity, nationhood or legitimate entitlement to the land in which the Palestinian people have lived throughout their recorded history.

The **second** is the myth of Israeli democracy. Innumerable newspaper stories or television references to the Israeli state are followed by the assertion that it is the only "real" democracy in the Middle East. In fact, Israel is as democratic as the apartheid state of South Africa. Civil liberty, due process and the most basic human rights are by law denied those who do not meet racial, religious criteria.

The **third** myth is that of "security" as the motor force of Israeli foreign policy. Zionists maintain that their state must be the fourth largest military power in the world because Israel has been forced to defend itself against imminent menace from primitive, hate-consumed Arab masses only recently dropped from the trees.

The **fourth** myth is that of Zionism as the moral legatee of the victims of the Holocaust. This is at once the most pervasive and insidious of the myths about Zionism. Ideologues for the Zionist movement have wrapped themselves in the collective shroud of the six million Jews who fell victim to Nazi mass murder. The bitter and cruel irony of this false claim is that the Zionist movement itself actively colluded with Nazism from its inception.

To most people it appears anomalous that the Zionist movement, which forever invokes the horror of the Holocaust, should have collaborated actively with the most vicious enemy ever faced by the Jews. The record, however, reveals not merely common interests but a deep ideological affinity rooted in the extreme chauvinism which they share.

CHAPTER TWO

Zionist Objectives

The objective of Zionism has never been merely to colonize Palestine—as was the goal of classical colonial and imperial movements during the 19th and 20th centuries. The design of European colonialism in Africa and Asia was, essentially, to exploit indigenous peoples as cheap labor while extracting natural resources for exorbitant profit.

What distinguishes Zionism from other colonial movements is the relationship between the settlers and the people to be conquered. The avowed purpose of the Zionist movement was not merely to exploit the Palestinian people but to disperse and dispossess them. The intent was to *replace* the indigenous population with a new settler community, to eradicate the farmers, artisans and town-dwellers of Palestine and *substitute* an entirely new workforce composed of the settler population.

In denying the existence of the Palestinian people, Zionism sought to create the political climate for their removal, not only from their land but from history. When acknowledged at all, the Palestinians were re-invented as a semi-savage, nomadic remnant. Historical records were falsified—a procedure begun during the last quarter of the 19th century but continuing to this day in such pseudo-historical writings as Joan Peters' "From Time Immemorial."

The Zionist movement would seek alternative imperial sponsors for this bloody enterprise; among them the Ottoman Empire, Imperial Germany, the British Raj, French colonialism and Czarist Russia. Zionist plans for the Palestinian people anticipated the Ottoman solution for the Armenians, who would be slaughtered in the first sustained genocide of the 20th century.

Zionist Plans for the Palestinian People

From its inception, the Zionist movement sought the "Armenianization" of the Palestinian people. Like the Native Americans, the Palestinians were regarded as "a people too many." The logic was elimination; the record was to be one of genocide.

This was no less true of the Labor Zionist movement, which sought to provide a "socialist" patina for the colonial enterprise. One of the principal theorists of Labor Zionism, a founder of the Zionist party Ha'Poel Ha'Tzair (The Young Worker) and a supporter of Poale Zion (Workers of Zion), was Aaron David Gordon.

Walter Laqueur acknowledges in his "History of Zionism" that, "A.D. Gordon and his comrades wanted every tree and every bush to be planted by Jewish 'pioneers.'"[14]

Gordon coined the slogan "conquest of labor" ["Kibbush avodah"]. He called upon Jewish capitalists, and the Rothschild plantation managers, who had obtained land from absentee Turkish landlords over the heads of the Palestinian people, "to hire Jews and only Jews." He organized boycotts of any Zionist enterprise which failed to employ Jews exclusively, and prepared strikes against the Rothschild colonists, who allowed Arab peasants to sharecrop or to work, even as cheap labor.

Thus, the "Labor Zionists" employed the methods of the workers' movement to prevent the use of Arab labor; their objective was not exploitation but usurpation.

Palestinian Society

There were over one thousand villages in Palestine at the turn of the 19th century. Jerusalem, Haifa, Gaza, Jaffa, Nablus, Acre, Jericho, Ramle, Hebron and Nazareth were flourishing towns. The hills were painstakingly terraced. Irrigation ditches crisscrossed the land. The citrus orchards, olive groves and grains of Palestine were known throughout the world. Trade, crafts, textiles, cottage industry and agricultural production abounded.

Eighteenth and 19th century travellers' accounts are replete with the data, as were the scholarly quarterly reports published in the 19th century by the British Palestine Exploration Fund.

In fact, it was precisely the social cohesiveness and stability of Palestinian society which led Lord Palmerston, in 1840, when Britain had established a consulate in Jerusalem, to propose, presciently, the founding of a European Jewish settler colony to "preserve the larger interests of the British Empire."[15]

Palestinian society, if suffering from the collaboration of feudal landowners [effendi] with the Ottoman Empire, was nevertheless productive and culturally diverse, with a peasantry quite conscious of its social role. The Palestinian peasants and urban dwellers had made a clear, strongly felt distinction between the Jews who lived amongst them and would-be colonists, dating from the 1820's, when the 20,000 Jews of Jerusalem were wholly integrated and accepted in Palestinian society.

When the colonists at Petah Tikvah sought to push the peasants off the land, in 1886, they were met with organized resistance, but Jewish workers in neighboring villages and communities were wholly unaffected. When the Armenians escaping the Turkish genocide settled in Palestine they were welcomed. The genocide was ominously defended by Vladimir Jabotinsky and other Zionists in their attempts to obtain Turkish support.

In fact, until the Balfour Declaration [1917], the Palestinian response to Zionist settlements was unwisely tolerant. There was no organized Jew-hatred in Palestine, no massacres such as the Czar and Polish anti-Semites prepared, no racist counterpart in the Palestinian response to armed colonists (who used force wherever possible to drive Palestinians from the land). Not even spontaneous riots, expressing pent up Palestinian rage at the steady theft of their land, were directed at Jews as such.

Courting Imperial Favor

In 1896, Theodor Herzl set forth his plan for inducing the Ottoman Empire to grant Palestine to the Zionist movement:

"Supposing his Majesty the Sultan were to give us Palestine; we could, in return, undertake to regulate the finances of Turkey. We should there form an outpost of civilization as opposed to barbarism."[16]

By 1905, the Seventh World Zionist Congress had to acknowledge that the Palestinian people were organizing a political movement for national independence from the Ottoman Empire—a threat not merely to Turkish rule but to Zionist designs.

Speaking at this Congress, Max Nordau, a prominent Zionist leader, set forth Zionist concerns:

"The movement which has taken hold of a great part of the Arab people may easily take a direction which may cause harm in Palestine. ... The Turkish government may feel itself compelled to defend its reign in Palestine and Syria with armed force. ... In these circumstances, Turkey can be convinced that it will be important for her to have in Palestine and Syria a strong and well-organized group which ...

will resist any attack on the authority of the Sultan and defend his authority with all its might."[17]

As the Kaiser undertook to forge an alliance with Turkey as part of his contest with Britain and France for control of the Middle East, the Zionist movement made similar overtures to Imperial Germany. The Kaiser took nearly ten years in his on-and-off dealings with the Zionist leadership to formulate a plan for a Jewish state under Ottoman auspices which would have as its principal task the eradication of the Palestinian anti-colonial resistance and the securing of the interests of Imperial Germany in the region.

By 1914, however, the World Zionist Organization was already far advanced in its parallel bid to enlist the British Empire to undertake the break-up of the Ottoman Empire with Zionist assistance. Chaim Weizmann, who was to become president of the World Zionist Organization, made an important public announcement:

"We can reasonably say that should Palestine fall within the British sphere of influence, and should Britain encourage Jewish settlement there, as a British dependency, we could have in twenty to thirty years a million Jews out there, perhaps more; they would develop the country, bring back civilization to it and form a very effective guard for the Suez Canal."[18]

The Balfour Declaration

Weizmann secured from the British what the Zionist leaders had sought simultaneously from the Ottoman and German Imperial governments. On November 2, 1917, the Balfour Declaration was issued. It stated, in part:

"His Majesty's Government view with favor the establishment in Palestine of a national home for the Jewish People, and will use their best endeavors to facilitate the achievement of this object...."[19]

The Zionists were cynical in the delineation of their claim to Palestine. One moment they would assert that Palestine was a wasteland visited by occasional nomads; in the next breath they proposed to subjugate the very Palestinian population they had attempted to render invisible. A.D. Gordon, himself, repeatedly declared that the Palestinians whom, he insisted did not exist, should be prevented, by force from cultivating the soil.

This translated into the total expulsion of non-Jews from the Jewish "fatherland." A like description informed pronouncements by

British and Zionist leaders in their plans for the Palestinian population. By the time of the Balfour Declaration, British imperial armies had occupied most of the Ottoman Empire in the Middle East, having enlisted Arab leaders to fight the Turks under British direction in exchange for British assurances of "self-determination."

While the Zionists in their propaganda insisted that Palestine was unpopulated, in their dealings with their imperial sponsors they made clear that subjugation was the order of the day and offered themselves as the instrument.

The British responded in kind. The Balfour Declaration also contained a passage intended to lull Arab feudal leaders shocked by the treachery of the British Empire in handing over to the Zionists the very land in which Arab self-determination had been promised:

"it being clearly understood that nothing shall be done which may prejudice the civil and religious rights of existing non-Jewish communities in Palestine...."[20]

The British had for years used the Zionist leadership to enlist support for its war against Imperial Germany from all the major Jewish capitalists and banking concerns in the United States and Great Britain. With Weizmann they prepared to use Zionist colonization of Palestine as the instrument for political control over the Palestinian population.

The land without a people for a people without a land was in fact a country in ferment against colonial subjugation. Former Prime Minister and Foreign Secretary Arthur Balfour, himself, was brutally explicit in memoranda for the eyes of officials, despite the lip service for public consumption about the "civil and religious rights of the non-Jewish [sic] communities in Palestine."

"Zionism, be it right or wrong, good or bad is rooted in present needs, in future hopes of far profounder import than the desires of the 700,000-plus Arabs who now inhabit that ancient land."[21]

The South African Connection

There is a particular dimension to this secret consort between Balfour and the Zionist leadership to betray the aspirations of the Palestinian people. It was Weizmann's close friend and future Prime Minister of South Africa, General Jan Smuts, who, as South African delegate to the British War Cabinet during World War I, helped push the British government to adopt the Balfour Declaration and to make a commitment to construct a Zionist colony under British direction.

The relationship between the Zionist movement and the South African settlers had evolved earlier, as had the friendship between General Smuts and Chaim Weizmann. By the turn of the century, a large Jewish population, primarily from Lithuania, had settled in South Africa. The Zionist movement regarded this population as particularly susceptible to Zionist ideas because of their already established settler status in South Africa. Zionist leaders travelled constantly to South Africa seeking political and financial support.

N. Kirschner, former chairperson of the South African Zionist Federation, provides a vivid account of the intimate interaction between Zionist and South African leaders, the identification of Zionists like Weizmann and Herzl with the South African conception of a racially distinct colonizing populace, and the importance of a virtual pact between the two movements.[22]

In identifying Zionism with South African settler ideology, Chaim Weizmann was following the early admiration expressed by Theodor Herzl, the founder of political Zionism, for the quintessential colonial ideologue, Sir Cecil Rhodes. Herzl attempted to model his own political future on the achievements of Rhodes:

"Naturally, there are big differences between Cecil Rhodes and my humble self, the personal ones very much in my disfavor; the objective ones are greatly in favor of the Zionist movement."[23]

Herzl advocated achieving Zionist dispersal of the Palestinians by using the methods pioneered by Rhodes, and he urged the formation of a Jewish counterpart to a colonial chartered company, an amalgam of colonial and entrepreneurial exploitation:

"The Jewish Company is partly modelled on the lines of a great acquisition company. It might be called a Jewish Chartered Company, though it cannot exercise sovereign power, and has no other than purely colonial tasks."[24]

"The poorest will go first to cultivate the soil. In accordance with a preconceived plan they will construct roads, bridges, railways and telegraph installations, regulate rivers and build their own habitations; their labor will create trade, trade will create markets, and markets will attract new settlers."[25]

By 1934, a major group of South African investors and large capitalists had established Africa-Israel Investments to purchase land in Palestine. The company still exists after 54 years with South Africans as joint stockholders, the assets held by Israel's Bank Leumi.[26]

The Iron Wall

The tension between the claim that the land was empty and the demand that the "non-existent" inhabitants be ruthlessly subjugated was less acute when Zionists discussed strategy among themselves. The reality of what was necessary to colonize Palestine took precedence over propaganda.

One of the ideological forbears of Zionism, Vladimir Jabotinsky, is known as the founder of "Revisionist Zionism," the Zionist current which had little patience with the liberal and socialist facade employed by the "labor" Zionists. [Revisionist Zionism is represented today by Menachem Begin and Yitzhak Shamir.]

In 1923 Jabotinsky wrote "The Iron Wall," which could be called a benchmark essay for the entire Zionist movement. He set forth bluntly the essential premises of Zionism which had, indeed, been laid out before, if not as eloquently, by Theodor Herzl, Chaim Weizmann and others. Jabotinsky's reasoning has been cited and reflected in subsequent Zionist advocacy—from nominal "left" to so-called "right." He wrote as follows:

"There can be no discussion of voluntary reconciliation between us and the Arabs, not now, and not in the foreseeable future. All well-meaning people, with the exception of those blind from birth, understood long ago the complete impossibility of arriving at a voluntary agreement with the Arabs of Palestine for the transformation of Palestine from an Arab country to a country with a Jewish majority. Each of you has some general understanding of the history of colonization. Try to find even one example when the colonization of a country took place with the agreement of the native population. Such an event has never occurred.

"The natives will always struggle obstinately against the colonists— and it is all the same whether they are cultured or uncultured. The comrades in arms of [Hernán] Cortez or [Francisco] Pizarro conducted themselves like brigands. The Redskins fought with uncompromising fervor against both evil and good-hearted colonizers. The natives struggled because any kind of colonization anywhere at anytime is inadmissible to any native people.

"Any native people view their country as their national home, of which they will be complete masters. They will never voluntarily allow a new master. So it is for the Arabs. Compromisers among us try to convince us that the Arabs are some kind of fools who can be tricked with hidden formulations of our basic goals. I flatly refuse to accept this view of the Palestinian Arabs.

"They have the precise psychology that we have. They look upon Palestine with the same instinctive love and true fervor that any Aztec looked upon his Mexico or any Sioux upon his prairie. Each people will struggle against colonizers until the last spark of hope that they can avoid the dangers of conquest and colonization is extinguished. The Palestinians will struggle in this way until there is hardly a spark of hope.

"It matters not what kind of words we use to explain our colonization. Colonization has its own integral and inescapable meaning understood by every Jew and by every Arab. Colonization has only one goal. This is in the nature of things. To change that nature is impossible. It has been necessary to carry on colonization against the will of the Palestinian Arabs and the same condition exists now.

"Even an agreement with non-Palestinians represents the same kind of fantasy. In order for Arab nationalists of Baghdad and Mecca and Damascus to agree to pay so serious a price they would have to refuse to maintain the Arab character of Palestine.

"We cannot give any compensation for Palestine, neither to the Palestinians nor to other Arabs. Therefore, a voluntary agreement is inconceivable. All colonization, even the most restricted, must continue in defiance of the will of the native population. Therefore, it can continue and develop only under the shield of force which comprises an *Iron Wall* through which the local population can never break through. This is our Arab policy. To formulate it any other way would be hypocrisy.

"Whether through the Balfour Declaration or the Mandate, external force is a necessity for establishing in the country conditions of rule and defense through which the local population, regardless of what it wishes, will be deprived of the possibility of impeding our colonization, administratively or physically. Force must play its role—with strength and without indulgence. In this, there are no meaningful differences between our militarists and our vegetarians. One prefers an *Iron Wall* of Jewish bayonets; the other an *Iron Wall* of English bayonets.

"To the hackneyed reproach that this point of view is unethical, I answer, 'absolutely untrue.' This is our ethic. There is no other ethic. As long as there is the faintest spark of hope for the Arabs to impede us, they will not sell these hopes—not for any sweet words nor for any tasty morsel, because this is not a rabble but a people, a living people. And no people makes such enormous concessions on such fateful questions, except when there is no hope left, until we have removed every opening visible in the *Iron Wall*."27

The Metaphor of Iron

The theme and imagery of coercive iron and steel evoked by Vladimir Jabotinsky was to be taken up by the nascent national socialist movement in Germany, even as Jabotinsky had, in turn, been inspired by Benito Mussolini. The mystical invocation of iron will in the service of martial and chauvinist conquest united Zionist, colonial and fascist ideologues. It sought its legitimacy in legends of a conquering past.

Cecil B. de Mille's "Samson and Delilah" was more than a Hollywood biblical romance about the perfidy of woman and the virtue of manly strength. It carried, as well, the authoritarian values of the novel from which it was adopted, Vladimir Jabotinsky's "Samson," which trumpeted the necessity of brute force if the Israelites were to conquer the Philistines.

"'Shall I give our people a message from you?' Samson thought for a while, and then said slowly: 'The first word is iron. They must get iron. They must give everything they have for iron—their silver and wheat, oil and wine and flocks, even their wives and daughters. All for iron! There is nothing in the world more valuable than iron.'"28

Jabotinsky, the siren of "an iron wall through which the local population can not break through" and of "the iron law of every colonizing movement ... armed force," found his call echoed in major Zionist forays against victim peoples in the decades to come.

Israel's current Minister of Defense, Yitzhak Rabin, launched the 1967 war as Chief of Staff with "Iron Will." As Prime Minister in 1975 and 1976 he declared the policy of *Hayad Barzel*, the "Iron Hand," in the West Bank. Over 300,000 Palestinians were to pass through Israeli prisons under conditions of sustained and institutionalized torture exposed by the *Sunday Times* of London and denounced by Amnesty International.

His successor as Chief of Staff, Raphael Eitan, imposed the "Iron Arm"—*Zro'aa Barzel*—on the West Bank, and assassination was added to the repressive arsenal. On July 17, 1982, the Israeli cabinet met to prepare what the London *Sunday Times* would term "this carefully pre-planned military operation to purge the camps, called *Moah Bar-*

zel or "Iron Brain." The camps were Sabra and Shatila and the operation "was familiar to Sharon and Begin, part of Sharon's larger plan discussed by the Israeli cabinet."[29]

When Yitzhak Rabin, who had supported the Revisionist Likud in Lebanon during the war, became Shimon Peres' Minister of Defense in the current "national unity" government, he launched in Lebanon and the West Bank the policy of *Egrouf Barzel*, the "Iron Fist." It is the "Iron Fist" which Rabin again cited as the basis for his policy of all-out repression and collective punishment during the 1987-1988 Palestinian uprising in the West Bank and Gaza.

It's interesting to recall, as well, that Jabotinsky located his colonial impulse in the doctrine of the purity of blood. Jabotinsky spelled this out in his "Letter on Autonomy:"

"It is impossible for a man to become assimilated with people whose blood is different than his own. In order to become assimilated, he must change his body, he must become one of them, in blood. There can be no assimilation. We shall never allow such things as mixed marriage because the preservation of national integrity is impossible except by means of racial purity and for that purpose we shall have this territory where our people will constitute the racially pure inhabitants."

This theme was further elaborated by Jabotinsky:

"The source of national feeling ... lies in a man's blood ... in his racio-physico type and in that alone. ... A man's spiritual outlook is primarily determined by his physical structure. For that reason we do not believe in spiritual assimilation. It is inconceivable, from the physical point of view, that a Jew born to a family of pure Jewish blood can become adapted to the spiritual outlook of a German or a Frenchman. He may be wholly imbued with that German fluid, but the nucleus of his spiritual structure will always remain Jewish."[30]

The adoption of chauvinist doctrines of racial purity and the logic of the blood were not confined to Jabotinsky or to the revisionists. The liberal philosopher, Martin Buber, located his Zionism equally within the framework of European racist doctrine:

"The deepest layers of our being are determined by blood; our innermost thinking and our will are colored by it."[31]

How was this to be implemented?

CHAPTER THREE

Colonizing Palestine

In 1917, there were 56,000 Jews in Palestine and 644,000 Palestinian Arabs. In 1922, there were 83,794 Jews and 663,000 Arabs. In 1931, there were 174,616 Jews and 750,000 Arabs.[32]

Collaborating with British Colonialism

With the forging of a tacit alliance with the British, the Zionists now received support on the ground for their conquest of the land. The process was described by the Palestinian poet and Marxist analyst, Ghassan Kanafani:

"Despite the fact that a large share of Jewish capital was allocated to rural areas, and despite the presence of British imperialist military forces and the immense pressure exerted by the administrative machine in favor of the Zionists, the latter achieved only minimal results with respect to the settlement of land.

"They, nevertheless, seriously damaged the status of the Arab rural population. Ownership by Jewish groups of urban and rural land rose from 300,000 dunums in 1929 [67,000 acres] to 1,250,000 dunums in 1930 [280,000 acres]. The purchased land was insignificant from the point of view of mass colonization and of the settlement of the "Jewish problem." But the expropriation of one million dunums—almost one third of the agricultural land—led to a severe impoverishment of Arab peasants and Bedouins.

"By 1931, 20,000 peasant families had been evicted by the Zionists. Furthermore, agricultural life in the underdeveloped world, and the Arab world in particular, is not merely a mode of production, but equally a way of social, religious and ritual life. Thus, in addition to the loss of land, Arab rural society was being destroyed by the process of colonization."[33]

British imperialism promoted the economic destabilization of the indigenous Palestinian economy. The Mandatory Government granted a privileged status to Jewish capital, awarding it 90% of the concessions in Palestine. This enabled the Zionists to gain control of the economic infrastructure (road projects, Dead Sea minerals, electricity, ports, etc.).

By 1935, Zionists controlled 872 of a total of 1,212 industrial firms in Palestine. Imports related to Zionist industries were exempted from taxes. Discriminatory work laws were passed against the Arab workforce resulting in large scale unemployment and a substandard existence for those who were able to find employment.

The 1936 Uprising

Loss of land and repression heightened Palestinian awareness of the fate intended for them and fueled a great uprising which lasted from 1936 to 1939.

The revolt assumed the form of civil disobedience and armed insurrection. Peasants left their villages to join fighting units which were formed in the mountains. Arab nationalists from Syria and Jordan soon entered the struggle.

The decision to withhold taxes was taken May 7, 1936, at a conference attended by one hundred fifty delegates representing all sectors of the population and a general strike swept Palestine.

British reaction was immediate and harsh. Martial law was declared July 30, 1936—approximately five months after the uprising had begun—and widespread repression was unleashed. Anyone suspected of organizing or sympathizing with the general strike or other resistance was detained. Houses were blown up throughout Palestine. A large section of the city of Jaffa was destroyed by the British on June 18, 1936, rendering 6,000 people homeless. Homes, as well, in the surrounding communities were demolished.

Britain sent large numbers of troops to Palestine to quell the revolt (estimated at 20,000). By the end of 1937 and the begining of 1938, however, British forces were losing control to the armed popular revolt.

The Zionists as Police Enforcers

It was at this point that the British began to rely on the Zionists who provided them with a unique resource they had never tapped in any of their colonies: a local force which had made common cause with British colonialism and was highly mobilized against the indigenous population. If before this the Zionists had handled many of the tasks of reprisal, they now played a larger role in the escalated repression which was to include mass arrests, assassinations and executions. In 1938, 5,000 Palestinians were imprisoned, of whom 2,000 were sentenced to long terms of imprisonment; 148 people were executed by hanging and over 5,000 homes were demolished.[34]

Zionist forces were integrated with British intelligence and became the police enforcers of draconian British rule. A "quasi-police force" was established to provide cover for the armed Zionist presence encouraged by the British. There were 2,863 recruits to the quasi-police force, 12,000 men were organized in the Haganah, and 3,000 in Jabotinsky's National Military Organization (Irgun).[35] In the summer of 1937 the quasi-police force was named the "Defense of the Jewish Colonies," and later the "Colony Police."

Ben Gurion called the quasi-police force an ideal "framework" for the training of the Haganah. Charles Orde Wingate, the British officer in charge, was, in essence, the founder of the Israeli army. He trained such figures as Moshe Dayan in terrorism and assassination.

By 1939, Zionist forces working with the British rose to 14,411 organized into ten well-armed groups of Colony Police, each commanded by a British officer, with an official of the Jewish Agency as second in command. By the spring of 1939, the Zionist force included sixty-three mechanized units, each consisting of eight to ten men.

The Peel Report

A Royal Commission was established in 1937, under the direction of Lord Peel, to determine the causes of the 1936 revolt. The Peel Commission concluded that the two primary factors were Palestinian desire for national independence and Palestinian fear of the establishment of a Zionist colony on their land. The Peel Report analyzed a series of other factors with uncommon candor. These were:

1) The spread of the Arab nationalist spirit outside Palestine

2) Increasing Jewish immigration after 1933

3) The ability of the Zionists to dominate public opinion in Britain because of the tacit support of the government

4) Lack of Arab confidence in the good intentions of the British government

5) Palestinian fear of continued land purchases by Jews from absentee feudal landowners who sold off their landholdings and evicted the Palestinian peasants who had worked the land

6) The evasiveness of the Mandatory government about its intentions regarding Palestinian sovereignty.

The national movement consisted of the urban bourgeoisie, feudal landowners, religious leaders and representatives of peasants and workers.

Its demands were:

1) An immediate stop to Zionist immigration

2) Cessation and prohibition of the transfer of the ownership of Arab lands to Zionist colonists

3) The establishment of a democratic government in which Palestinians would have the controlling voice.[36]

Analysis of the Revolt

Ghassan Kanafani described the uprising:

"The real cause of the revolt was the fact that the acute conflict involved in the transformation of Palestinian society from an Arab agricultural-feudal-clerical one into a Jewish (Western) industrial bourgeois one, had reached its climax. ... The process of establishing the roots of colonialism and transforming it from a British mandate into Zionist settler colonialism ... reached its climax in the mid-thirties, and in fact the leadership of the Palestinian nationalist movement was obliged to adopt a certain form of armed struggle because it was no longer able to exercise its leadership at a time when the conflict had reached decisive proportions."[37]

The failure of the Mufti and other religious leaders, of feudal land owners and the nascent bourgeoisie to support the peasants and workers to the end, enabled the colonial regime and the Zionists to crush the rebellion after three years of heroic struggle. In this the British were aided decisively by the treachery of the traditional Arab regimes, who were dependent upon their colonial sponsors.

The Palestinian national struggle has been continuous since 1918 and has been accompanied by one or another form of organized armed resistance. It has also included civil disobedience, general strikes, non-payment of taxes, refusal to carry identity cards, boycotts and demonstrations.

CHAPTER FOUR

Tragic Consequences

In 1947, there were 630,000 Jews and 1,300,000 Palestinian Arabs. Thus, by the time of the United Nations partition of Palestine in 1947, the Jews were 31% of the population.[38]

The decision to partition Palestine, promoted by the leading imperialist powers and Stalin's Soviet Union, gave 54% of the fertile land to the Zionist movement. But before the state of Israel was established, the Irgun and Haganah seized three-quarters of the land and expelled virtually all the inhabitants.

In 1948, there were 475 Palestinian villages and towns. Of these, 385 were razed to the ground, reduced to rubble. Ninety remain, stripped of their land.

Removing the Mask

In 1940, Joseph Weitz, the head of the Jewish Agency's Colonization Department, which was responsible for the actual organization of settlements in Palestine, wrote:

"Between ourselves it must be clear that there is no room for both peoples together in this country. We shall not achieve our goal if the Arabs are in this small country. There is no other way than to transfer the Arabs from here to neighboring countries—all of them. Not one village, not one tribe should be left."[39]

Joseph Weitz elaborated upon the practical meaning of rendering Palestine "Jewish:"

"There are some who believe that the non-Jewish population, even in a high percentage, within our borders will be more effectively under our surveillance; and there are some who believe the contrary, i.e., that it is easier to carry out surveillance over the activities of a neighbor than over those of a tenant. [I] tend to support the latter view and have an additional argument: ...the need to sustain the character of the state which will henceforth be Jewish ... with a non-Jewish minority limited to fifteen percent. I had already reached this fundamental position as early as 1940 [and] it is entered in my diary."[40]

The "Koenig Report" stated this policy even more bluntly:

"We must use terror, assassination, intimidation, land confiscation and the cutting of all social services to rid the Galilee of its Arab population."[41]

Chairman Heilbrun of the Committee for the Re-election of General Shlomo Lahat, the mayor of Tel Aviv, declaimed: "We have to kill all the Palestinians unless they are resigned to live here as slaves."[42]

These are the words of Uri Lubrani, Israeli Prime Minister David Ben Gurion's special adviser on Arab Affairs, in 1960: "We shall reduce the Arab population to a community of woodcutters and waiters."[43]

Raphael Eitan, Chief of Staff of the Israeli Armed Forces stated:
"We declare openly that the Arabs have no right to settle on even one centimeter of Eretz Israel. ... Force is all they do or ever will understand. We shall use the ultimate force until the Palestinians come crawling to us on all fours."[44]

Eitan elaborated before the Knesset's Foreign Affairs and Defense Committee:

"When we have settled the land, all the Arabs will be able to do will be to scurry around like drugged roaches in a bottle."[45]

Ben Gurion and the Final Aim

The territorial ambitions of Zionism were clearly spelled out by David Ben Gurion in a speech to a Zionist meeting on October 13, 1936: "We do not suggest that we announce now our final aim which is far reaching—even more so than the Revisionists who oppose Partition. I am unwilling to abandon the great vision, the final vision which is an organic, spiritual and ideological component of my ... Zionist aspirations."[46]

In the same year, Ben Gurion wrote in a letter to his son:

"A partial Jewish State is not the end, but only the beginning. I am certain that we can not be prevented from settling in the other parts of the country and the region."

In 1937, he declaimed:

"The boundaries of Zionist aspirations are the concern of the Jewish people and no external factor will be able to limit them."[47]

In 1938, he was more explicit: "The boundaries of Zionist aspiration," he told the World Council of Poale Zion in Tel Aviv, "include southern Lebanon, southern Syria, today's Jordan, all of Cis-Jordan [West Bank] and the Sinai."[48]

Ben Gurion formulated Zionist strategy very clearly:

"After we become a strong force as the result of the creation of the state, we shall abolish partition and expand to the whole of Palestine. The state will only be a stage in the realization of Zionism and its task is to prepare the ground for our expansion. The state will have to preserve order—not by preaching but with machine guns."[49]

In May of 1948 he presented his strategic aims to the General Staff. "We should prepare to go over to the offensive. Our aim is to smash Lebanon, Trans-Jordan, and Syria. The weak point is Lebanon, for the Moslem regime is artificial and easy for us to undermine. We shall establish a Christian state there, and then we will smash the Arab Legion, eliminate Trans-Jordan; Syria will fall to us. We then bomb and move on and take Port Saïd, Alexandria, and Sinai."[50]

When General Yigal Allon asked Ben Gurion, "What is to be done with the population of Lydda and Ramle?"—some 50,000 inhabitants—Ben Gurion, according to his biographer, waved his hand and said, "Drive them out!"[51]

Yitzhak Rabin, the current Defense Minister, carried out this edict. In Lydda and Ramle, no remnants of Palestinian dwellings remain. Today this area is occupied entirely by the Jewish settler population.

Michael Bar Zohar, in his biography of David Ben Gurion, describes Ben Gurion's first visit to Nazareth. "Ben Gurion looked around in astonishment and said, 'Why are there so many Arabs, why didn't you drive them out?'"

The Palestinians *were* indeed driven out. Between November 29, 1947, when the United Nations partitioned Palestine, and May 15, 1948, when the State was formally proclaimed, the Zionist army and militia had seized 75% of Palestine, forcing 780,000 Palestinians out of the country.

The Butchery Begins: Deir Yasin

The process was one of sustained slaughter as village after village was wiped out. The killing was intended to cause people to flee for their lives.

The commander of the Haganah, Zvi Ankori, described what happened: "I saw cut off genitalia and women's crushed stomachs. ... It was direct murder."[52]

Menachem Begin gloated over the impact throughout Palestine of the Nazi-like operations he commanded at Deir Yasin. Lehi and IZL

Commandos stormed the village of Deir Yasin on April 9, 1948, slaughtering 254 men, women and children.

"A legend of terror spread amongst Arabs who were seized with panic at the mention of our Irgun soldiers. It was worth half a dozen battalions to the forces of Israel. Arabs throughout the country ... were seized with limitless panic and started to flee for their lives. This mass flight soon developed into a maddened, uncontrollable stampede. Of the 800,000 Arabs who lived on the present territory of the state of Israel, only some 165,000 are still there. The political and economic significance of this development can hardly be overestimated."[53]

The implementation of this program was carried out in part by Menachem Begin and in part by his future successor as Prime Minister, Yitzhak Shamir, as military commanders of the Irgun and the Lohamei Herut Israel (Lehi), i.e., Fighters for the Freedom of Israel. Inhabitants were force marched in blood-soaked clothing through the streets of Jerusalem to jeering on-lookers, before disappearing.

Eyewitness Accounts

The eyewitness accounts of these events foreshadowed the fate of the Palestinian people.

"It was noon when the battle ended and the shooting stopped. Things had become quiet, but the village had not surrendered. The IZL (Irgun) and Lehi (Stern Gang) irregulars left the places in which they had been hiding and started carrying out clean-up operations in the houses. They fired with all the arms they had, and threw explosives into the buildings. They also shot everyone they saw in the houses, including women and children—indeed the commanders made no attempt to check the disgraceful acts of slaughter. I myself and a number of inhabitants begged the commanders to give orders to their men to stop shooting, but our efforts were unsuccessful. In the meantime, some twenty-five men had been brought out of the houses: they were loaded into a freight truck and led in a 'victory parade,' like a Roman triumph, through to Mahaneh Yehudah and Zikhron Yosef quarters [of Jerusalem]. At the end of the parade they were taken to a stone quarry between Giv'at Shaul and Deir Yasin and shot in cold blood. The fighters then put the women and children who were still alive on a truck and took them to the Mandelbaum Gate."[54]

The director of the International Red Cross in Palestine, Jacques de

Reynier, attempted to intervene as word of the slaughter spread. His personal testimony is as follows:

"...The Commander of the Irgun detachment did not seem willing to receive me. At last he arrived, young, distinguished, and perfectly correct, but there was a peculiar glitter in his eyes, cold and cruel. According to him the Irgun had arrived twenty-four hours earlier and ordered the inhabitants by loudspeaker to evacuate all houses and surrender: the time given to obey the order was a quarter of an hour. 'Some of these miserable people had come forward and were taken prisoner, to be released later in the direction of the Arab lines. The rest, not having obeyed the order, had met the fate they deserved. But there was no point in exaggerating things, there were only a few dead, and they would be buried as soon as the 'clean-up' of the village was over. If I found any bodies, I could take them, but there were certainly no wounded.'

"This account made my blood run cold. I went back to the Jerusalem road and got an ambulance and a truck that I had alerted through the Red Shield. ... I reached the village with my convoy, and the firing stopped. The gang (Irgun) was wearing uniforms with helmets. All of them were young, some even adolescents, men and women, armed to the teeth: revolvers, machine-guns, hand grenades, and also cutlasses in their hands, most of them still blood-stained. A beautiful young girl with criminal eyes showed me hers, still dripping with blood; she displayed it like a trophy. This was the 'clean-up' team, that was obviously performing its task very conscientiously.

"I tried to go into a house. A dozen soldiers surrounded me, their machine-guns aimed at my body, and their officer forbade me to move. The dead, if any, would be brought to me, he said. I then flew into one of the most towering rages of my life, telling these criminals what I thought of their conduct, threatening them with everything I could think of, and then pushed them aside and went into the house.

"The first room was dark, everything was in disorder, but there was no one. In the second, amid disembowelled furniture and all sorts of debris, I found some bodies, cold. Here the 'clean-up' had been done with machine guns, then hand grenades. It had been finished off with knives, anyone could see that. The same thing in the next room, but as I was about to leave, I heard something like a sigh. I looked everywhere, turned over all the bodies, and eventually found a little foot, still warm. It was a little girl of ten, mutilated by a hand grenade, but still alive ... everywhere it was the same horrible sight ... there had been four hundred people in this village; about fifty of them had escaped and were still alive. All the rest had been deliberately massacred in cold blood for, as I observed for myself, this gang was admirably disciplined and only acted under orders.

"After another visit to Deir Yasin I went back to my office where I was visited by two gentlemen, well-dressed in civilian clothes, who had been waiting for me for more than an hour. They were the commander of the Irgun detachment and his aide. They had prepared a paper which they wanted me to sign. It was a statement to the effect that I had been very courteously received by them, and obtained all the facilities I had requested, in the accomplishment of my mission, and thanking them for the help I had received. As I showed signs of hesitation and even started to argue with them, they said that if I valued my life, I had better sign immediately. The only course open to me was to convince them that I did not value my life in the least."[55]

The Slaughter at Dueima

If the Deir Yasin massacre was carried out by the "rightist" Revisionist Zionist underground organizations, IZL and Lehi, like massacres occurred on a similar scale throughout the country. The massacre at Dueima in 1948 was perpetrated by the official Labor Zionist Israeli army, the Israel Defense Forces (Tzeva Haganah le-Israel or ZAHAL). The account of the massacre, as described by a soldier who participated in the horror, was published in *Davar*, the official Hebrew daily newspaper of the Labor-Zionist-run Histadrut General Federation of Workers:

"...They killed between eighty to one hundred Arab men, women and children. To kill the children they [soldiers] fractured their heads with sticks. There was not one home without corpses. The men and women of the villages were pushed into houses without food or water. Then the saboteurs came to dynamite them.

"One commander ordered a soldier to bring two women into a building he was about to blow up. ... Another soldier prided himself upon having raped an Arab woman before shooting her to death. Another Arab woman with her newborn baby was made to clean the place for a couple of days, and then they shot her and the baby. Educated and well-mannered commanders who were considered 'good guys' ... became base murderers, and this not in the storm of battle, but as a method of expulsion and extermination. The fewer the Arabs who remain, the better."[56]

The strategic value of the Deir Yasin massacre would be propounded widely over the years by Zionist leaders such as Eldad [Scheib] who, with Yitzhak Shamir and Nathan Yalin-Mor [Feldman], were in charge of Lehi. Speaking at a meeting in July 1967, his remarks were published in the well-known journal of opinion, *De'ot*, in Winter 1968:

"I have always said that if the deepest and profoundest hope symbolizing redemption is the rebuilding of the [Jewish] Temple ... then it is obvious that those mosques [al-Haram al-Sharif and al-Aqsa] will have, one way or another, to disappear one of these days. ... Had it not been for Deir Yasin, half a million Arabs would be living in the state of Israel [in 1948]. The state of Israel would not have existed. We must not disregard this, with full awareness of the responsibility involved. All wars are cruel. There is no way out of that. This country will either be Eretz Israel with an absolute Jewish majority and a small Arab minority, or Eretz Ishmael, and Jewish emigration will begin again if we do not expel the Arabs one way or another...."[57]

Murder in Gaza

The program of massacre did not end with the formation of the state. Meir Har Tzion's diary describes the massacres in the refugee camps and villages of Gaza during the early 1950's:

"The wide, dry riverbed glitters in the moonlight. We advance, carefully, along the mountain slope. Several houses can be seen. ... In the distance we can see three lights and hear the sounds of Arab music coming out of the homes immersed in darkness. We split up into three groups of four men each. Two groups make their way to the immense refugee camp (Al Burj) to the south of our position. The other group marches toward the lonely house in the flat area north of Wadi Gaza. We march forward, trampling over green fields, wading through water canals as the moon bathes us in its scintillating light. Soon, however, the silence will be shattered by bullets, explosions, and the screams of those who are now sleeping peacefully. We advance quickly and enter one of the houses—'Mann Haatha?' [Arabic for 'Who's there?']

"We leap towards the voices. Fearing and trembling, two Arabs are standing up against the wall of the building. They try to escape. I open fire. An ear-piercing scream fills the air. One man falls to the ground while his friend continues to run. Now we must act—we have no time to lose. We make our way from house to house as the Arabs scramble about in confusion.

"Machine guns rattle, their noise mixed with a terrible howling. We reach the main thoroughfare of the camp. The mob of fleeing Arabs grows larger. The other group attacks from the opposite direction. The thunder of our hand-grenades echoes in the distance. We receive an order to retreat. The attack has come to an end."[58]

Kibya and Commando Unit 101

Prime Minister Moshe Sharett (1954-55) gave the following account of the massacre at the village of Kibya in 1953 (October 18, 1953). Ariel Sharon personally commanded the action in which men, women and children were slaughtered in their homes.

"[In the cabinet meeting] I condemned the Kibya Affair that *exposed* us in front of the whole world as a gang of blood-suckers capable of massacres. ... I warned that this stain will stick to us and will not be washed away for years to come.

"It was decided that a communiqué on Kibya will be published and Ben Gurion was to write it. It is really a shameful deed. I inquired several times and each time I was solemnly assured that people would not find out how it had been done."[59]

Sharett noted in his Diary details of further massacres in Palestinian villages in 1955: "Public opinion, the army and the police have concluded that Arab blood can be freely shed. It must make the state appear in the eyes of the world as a savage state."[60]

Kafr Qasim: The Slaughter Continues

The massacre at Kafr Qasim followed the Zionist pattern. In October 1956, Israeli Brigadier Shadmi, the commander of a battalion on the Israeli-Jordanian border, ordered a night curfew imposed on the "minority" [Arab] villages under his command. These villages were inside the Israeli borders; thus, their inhabitants were Israeli citizens. Shadmi told the commander of a Frontier Guard unit, Major Melinki, that the curfew must be "extremely strict" and that "it would not be enough to arrest those who broke it—they must be shot." He added: "A dead man is better than the complications of detention."[61]

"He [Melinki] informed the assembled officers that ... their task was to impose the curfew in the minority villages from 1700 to 0600 [5 p.m. to 6 a.m.]. ... Anyone leaving his home, or anyone breaking the curfew should be shot dead. He added that there were to be no arrests and that if a number of people were killed in the night this would facilitate the imposition of the curfew during succeeding nights.

"Lieutenant Frankanthal asked him: 'What do we do with the wounded?' Melinki replied: 'Take no notice of them.'

"A section leader, then asked: 'What about women and children?' to which Melinki replied: 'No sentimentality.' When asked: 'What about people returning from their work?' Melinki answered: 'It will be just too bad for them, as the Commander said.'"

The perpetrators of the Kafr Qasim massacre—a commando unit of Ariel Sharon—Commando Unit 101—were all rewarded with medals and with promotions in the Israeli Defense Forces (IDF).

The genocidal methods needed to impose the colonial settler state within the pre-1967 borders of Israel are regarded as the model for dealing ultimately with the Palestinians in the post-1967 occupied territories. Aharon Yariv, former military intelligence chief and Minister of Information, stated at a public seminar in the Leonard Davis Institute for International Relations at the Hebrew University in Jerusalem that:

"There are opinions which advocate that a war situation be utilized in order to exile 700,000 to 800,000 Arabs. These opinions are widespread. Statements have been voiced on the matter and also instruments [apparatuses] have been prepared."[62]

CHAPTER FIVE

The Seizure of the Land

It is appropriate to review the pervasiveness of this murderous policy and its consequences. In the territory which came under Israeli occupation after Partition there were approximately 950,000 Palestinian Arabs. They inhabited nearly 500 villages and all the major cities, which included Tiberias, Safed, Nazareth, Shafa Amr, Acre, Haifa, Jaffa, Lydda, Ramle, Jerusalem, Majdal (Ashqelon), Isdud (Ashdod) and Beersheba.

After less than six months only 138,000 people remained. (Figures vary from 130,000 to 165,000.) The great majority of Palestinians were killed, forcibly expelled or fled in panic before slaughtering bands of Israeli army units.

Having thus eliminated most of the Palestinian inhabitants from the land of Palestine, the Israeli government undertook the systematic destruction of their homes and possessions. Nearly 400 villages and towns were razed to the ground during 1948 and 1949. More followed in the 1950's.

Moshe Dayan, former Chief of Staff and Minister of Defense, was uninhibited in his summary of the nature of Zionist colonization before students at the Israel Institute of Technology (The Techniyon):

"We came here to a country that was populated by Arabs, and we are building here a Hebrew, Jewish state. Instead of Arab villages, Jewish villages were established. You do not even know the names of these villages and I do not blame you, because these geography books no longer exist. Not only the books, but also the villages do not exist.

"Nahalal was established in place of Mahalul, Gevat in place of Jibta, Sarid in the place of Hanifas and Kafr Yehoushu'a in the place of Tel Shamam. There is not a single settlement that was not established in the place of a former Arab village."[64]

The following table was prepared by Israel Shahak, Chairperson of the Israeli League for Human and Civil Rights, under the heading "Arab Villages Destroyed in Israel."[65]

Destruction of Palestinian Arab Villages

Name of the District	Number of Villages Before '48	1988	Destroyed
Jerusalem	33	4	29
Bethlehem	7	0	7
Hebron	16	0	16
Jaffa	23	0	23
Ramle	31	0	31
Lydda	28	0	28
Jenin	8	4	4
Tulkarm	33	12	21
Haifa	43	8	35
Acre	52	32	20
Nazareth	26	20	6
Safad	75	7	68
Tiberias	26	3	23
Bisan	28	0	28
Gaza	46	0	46
Total	**475**	**90**	**385**

Shahak stresses that this documented list is incomplete because it is impossible to find numerous Arab communities and "tribes." Israeli official data characterize, for example, 44 Bedouin villages and towns as "tribes," to reduce, by census contrivance, the number of permanent Palestinian communities.

"Absentee" Property

With the expulsion of the Palestinians and the destruction of their towns and villages, vast amounts of property were seized under the rubric of the "Absentee Property Law" (1950).

Until 1947, Jewish land ownership in Palestine was some 6%. By the time the state was formally established, it had sequestered 90% of the land:

"Of the entire area of the state of Israel only about 300,000 to 400,000 dunums [67,000-89,000 acres] ... are state domain which the Israeli government took over from the Mandatory regime [British Mandate] [2%]. The J.N.F. (Jewish National Fund) and private Jewish owners possess under two million dunums [10%]. Almost all the rest [i.e., 88% of the 20,225,000 dunums (4,500,000 acres) within the 1949 armistice lines] belongs in law to Arab owners, many of whom have left the country."⁶⁶

The value of this stolen property was over $300 million—over thirty years ago. (Arab League estimates are ten times this amount.) In current dollars, this figure would have to be quadrupled.

"The U.N. Refugee Office estimated the value of Arab abandoned orchards, trees, movable and immovable property in the territory under Israeli jurisdiction was about 118-120 million Pounds Sterling, an average of £130 [$364] per refugee."⁶⁷

The seizure of Palestinian property was indispensable to make Israel a viable state. Between 1948 and 1953, 370 Jewish towns and settlements were established. Three hundred fifty were on "absentee" property. By 1954, some 35% of Israel's Jews lived on property confiscated from absentees and some 250,000 new immigrants settled in urban areas from which Palestinians had been expelled. Entire cities had been emptied of Palestinians, such as Jaffa, Acre, Lydda, Ramle, Bisan and Majdal (Ashqelon).

This plunder embraced 385 towns and villages in their entirety and large sections of 94 other cities and towns, containing 25% of all buildings in Israel. Ten thousand businesses and retail stores were handed over to Jewish settlers.

From 1948 to 1953—the period of greatest immigration—the economic importance to Israel of seized Arab property was decisive. The amount of cultivatable land seized from Palestinians driven from their country by massacre was two and one half times the total area of land granted the Zionists with the end of the mandate.

Virtually all citrus groves of Palestinians were seized—consisting of more than 240,000 dunums [53,000 acres]. By 1951, 1.25 million boxes of citrus from seized Arab groves were in Israeli hands—10% of the country's hard currency profits from export.

By 1951, 95% of all Israel's olive groves came from seized Palestinian land. Olive produce from stolen Palestinian groves represented Israel's third largest export—after citrus and diamonds.

One third of all stone production came from 52 seized Palestinian quarries.⁶⁸

Zionist mythology includes the claim that Zionist industry, dedication and skill transformed an otherwise barren desert land, neglected by its primitive nomadic Arab custodians, into a garden—making the desert bloom. Palestinian orchards, industry, rolling stock, factories, houses and possessions were pillaged after slaughtering conquest—the

Ship of State a vessel of pirates, its proper flag a skull and crossbones.

"Judaizing" the Land

The Jewish National Fund secured its first land in 1905. Its objectives were defined as the acquisition of land "for the purpose of settling Jews on such lands."[69] In May 1954, the Keren Kayemeth le-Israel, "Perpetual Fund for Israel," was incorporated in Israel and acquired all the assets of the Jewish National Fund.

In November 1961, the J.N.F. and the Israeli government signed a covenant based on legislation adopted in July 1960. It established the Israel Lands Administration. A uniform policy was legally in force on the 93% of the land in Israel under the aegis of the state, which was bound by the policies of the Keren Kayemeth le-Israel and the J.N.F.[69a]

As Prime Minister Levi Eshkol declared to the Knesset (Israeli Parliament) upon proposing that the state of Israel adopt the J.N.F.'s exclusive land policies: "The principle established as the basis of the Jewish National Fund ... will be established as a principle applying to state lands."[69b]

The Jewish National Fund is explicit on this point. It declared in J.N.F. Report 6:

"Following an agreement between the government of Israel and the J.N.F., the Knesset in 1960 enacted the *Basic Law: Israel-Lands* which gives legal effect to the ancient tradition of ownership of the land in perpetuity by the Jewish people—the principle on which the J.N.F. was founded. The same law extends that principle to the bulk of Israel's state domains."[69c]

Any relationship to this land was governed by the following condition spelled out in all leases pertaining to property:

"The lessee must be Jewish and must agree to execute all works connected with the cultivation of the holding only with Jewish labor."[70]

The consequence is that land cannot be leased to a non-Jew, nor can the lease be subleased, sold, mortgaged, given or bequeathed to a non-Jew. Non-Jews cannot be employed on the land nor in any work connected with cultivation. If these conditions are violated both fines and the abrogation of the lease, without any compensation, ensue.

What is particularly instructive is that these regulations are enforced not just by the J.N.F., but by the state under its laws. They apply to J.N.F. and all state lands, which consist, overwhelmingly, of "absentee" property.

Non-Jews Need Not Apply

In Israel these state lands are categorized as "national land." It means *Jewish,* not "Israeli" land. Employment of non-Jews is treated as illegal and an infraction of law. Because of a shortage of Jewish farm workers, and since Palestinians are paid a fraction of the wages allowed Jewish workers, some Jewish farmers (like former Defense Minister Ariel Sharon) employ Arabs. This practice is illegal! In 1974, the Minister of Agriculture denounced the practice as "a cancer."[71]

Settlements which sublease some land in sharecropping arrangements with Arabs are denounced. The spread of the practice, given the super-profits derived from cheap Palestinian labor, has been labelled "a plague" by the Ministry of Agriculture. The Settlement Department of the Jewish Agency has warned that such practices violate the law, the regulations of the Jewish Agency and of the Covenant between the Israeli State and the J.N.F.. The employment of non-Jews has been punished by fines and "a donation to a Special Fund."[72]

Israel Shahak has described this process as "a disgusting mixture of racial discrimination and financial corruption."

What all this reveals, however, is that the state of Israel employs all normal usage in a racist sense. The "people" means only Jews. An "immigrant" or a "settler" can only be a Jew. A settlement means a settlement for Jews alone. National land means Jewish land—not Israeli land.

Thus, law and rights, protections and the entitlement to employment or property pertain to Jews only. "Israeli" citizenship or nationality applies strictly to Jews in all the specific applications of their meaning and governance.

Since the definition of a Jew is entirely based upon orthodox religious dictate, "generations of maternal Jewish descent" is the prerequisite to enjoy the right to property, employment or protection under the law. There is no more pristine example of racist laws and procedures.

Using these same criteria, over 55% of the land and 70% of the water in the West Bank [territory occupied in 1967] have been seized for the benefit of 6% of the population—some 40,000 settlers among

800,000 Palestinians. In Gaza [territory occupied in 1967], 2,200 settlers have been given over 40% of the land. A half million Palestinians are confined in crowded camps and slums.

Thus, the practices universally decried in the post-1967 occupied territories are but the continuation of the very process wherein the Israeli state itself was established. The use of force, seizure of the land and exclusion of non-Jewish workers is central to Zionist theory and practice. Theodor Herzl promulgated this program on June 12, 1895:

"We shall ... spirit the penniless population across the border ... while denying it any employment in our country."[73]

The Racist Kibbutzim

Ironically, the Israeli institution about which the greatest illusions are entertained is the Kibbutz—a presumptive example of socialist cooperation.

As Israel Shahak stated:

"The Israeli organization which practices the greatest degree of racist exclusion is ... the Kibbutz. The majority of Israelis have been aware of the racist character of the Kibbutz as displayed not only against Palestinians but against all human beings who are not Jews, for quite a time."[74]

The Kibbutzim exist predominantly on seized Palestinian land. Non-Jews may not be members. Should "temporary workers" who are Christians become involved with Jewish women, they are forced to convert to Judaism in order to be members of a Kibbutz. Shahak reports:

"Christian candidates for Kibbutz membership through conversion have to promise to spit in the future when passing before a church or a cross."[75]

Today, some 93% of the land in what is called the state of Israel is controlled by the Israel Lands Administration under the guidelines of the Jewish National Fund. In order to be entitled to live on land, to lease land, or to work on land one must prove at least four generations of maternal Jewish descent.

If, in the United States, in order to live on land, lease it, rent it, or work it in any way, you had to prove that you did *not* have at least four generations of maternal Jewish descent, who would doubt the racist nature of such legislation?

CHAPTER SIX

Zionism and the Jews

If the colonization of Palestine has been characterized by a series of depredations, we should take a moment to examine the attitude of the Zionist movement not only toward its Palestinian victims (to which we shall return), but toward the Jews themselves.

Herzl himself wrote of the Jews in the following fashion: "I achieved a freer attitude toward anti-Semitism, which I now began to understand historically and to pardon. Above all, I recognized the emptiness and futility of trying to 'combat' anti-Semitism."[76]

The youth organization of the Zionists, Hashomer Hatzair (Young Guard) published the following: "A Jew is a caricature of a normal, natural human being, both physically and spiritually. As an individual in society he revolts and throws off the harness of social obligations, knows no order nor discipline."[77]

"The Jewish people," wrote Jabotinsky in the same vein, "is a very bad people; its neighbors hate it and rightly so ... its only salvation lies in a general immigration to the land of Israel."[78]

The founders of Zionism despaired of combatting anti-Semitism and, paradoxically, regarded the anti-Semites themselves as allies, because of a shared desire to remove the Jews from the countries in which they lived. Step by step, they assimilated the values of Jew-hatred and anti-Semitism, as the Zionist movement came to regard the anti-Semites themselves as their most reliable sponsors and protectors.

Theodor Herzl approached none other than Count Von Plehve, the author of the worst pogroms in Russia—the pogroms of Kishinev—with the following proposition: "Help me to reach the land [Palestine] sooner and the revolt [against Czarist rule] will end."[79]

Von Plehve agreed, and he undertook to finance the Zionist movement. He was later to complain to Herzl: "The Jews have been joining the revolutionary parties. We were sympathetic to your Zionist movement as long as it worked toward emigration. You don't have to justify the movement to me. You are preaching to a convert."[80]

Herzl and Weizmann offered to help guarantee Czarist interests in Palestine and to rid Eastern Europe and Russia of those "noxious and subversive Anarcho-Bolshevik Jews."

As we have noted, the same appeal was made by the Zionists to the Sultan of Turkey, the Kaiser in Germany, to French imperialism and to the British Raj.

Zionism and Fascism

The history of Zionism—largely suppressed—is sordid.

Mussolini set up squadrons of the Revisionist Zionist youth movement, Betar, in black shirts in emulation of his own Fascist bands. When Menachem Begin became chief of Betar, he preferred the brown shirts of the Hitler gangs, a uniform Begin and Betar members wore to all meetings and rallies—at which they greeted each other and opened and closed meetings with the fascist salute.

Simon Petilura was a Ukranian fascist who personally directed pogroms which killed 28,000 Jews in 897 separate pogroms. Jabotinsky negotiated an alliance with Petilura, proposing a Jewish police force to accompany Petilura's forces in their counter-revolutionary fight against the Red Army and the Bolshevik Revolution—a process involving the murder of peasant, worker and intellectual supporters of the revolution.

Collaborating with the Nazis

This strategy of enlisting Europe's virulent Jew-haters, and of aligning with the most vicious movements and regimes as financial and military patrons of a Zionist colony in Palestine, did not exclude the Nazis.

The Zionist Federation of Germany sent a memorandum of support to the Nazi Party on June 21, 1933. In it the Federation noted:

"...a rebirth of national life such as is occurring in German life ... must also take place in the Jewish national group.

"On the foundation of the new [Nazi] state which has established the principle of race, we wish so to fit our community into the total structure so that for us, too, in the sphere assigned to us, fruitful activity for the Fatherland is possible...."[81]

Far from repudiating this policy, the World Zionist Organization Congress in 1933 defeated a resolution calling for action against Hitler by a vote of 240 to 43.

During this very Congress, Hitler announced a trade agreement with the WZO's Anglo-Palestine Bank, breaking, thereby, the Jewish boycott of the Nazi regime at a time when the German economy was extremely vulnerable. It was the height of the Depression and people were wheeling barrels full of worthless German Marks. The World Zionist Organization broke the Jewish boycott and became the principal distributor of Nazi goods throughout the Middle East and Northern Europe. They established the Ha'avara, which was a bank in Palestine designed to receive monies from the German-Jewish bourgeoisie, with which sums Nazi goods were purchased in very substantial quantity.

Embracing the S.S.

Consequently, the Zionists brought Baron Von Mildenstein of the S.S. Security Service to Palestine for a six-month visit in support of Zionism. This visit led to a twelve-part report by Joseph Goebbels, Hitler's Minister of Propaganda, in *Der Angriff* (*The Assault*) in 1934 *praising* Zionism. Goebbels ordered a medallion struck with the Swastika on one side, and on the other, the Zionist Star of David.

In May 1935, Reinhardt Heydrich, the chief of the S.S. Security Service, wrote an article in which he separated Jews into "two categories." The Jews he favored were the Zionists: "Our good wishes together with our official good will go with them."[82]

In 1937, the Labor "socialist" Zionist militia, the Haganah (founded by Jabotinsky) sent an agent (Feivel Polkes) to Berlin offering to spy for the S.S. Security Service in exchange for the release of Jewish wealth for Zionist colonization. Adolf Eichmann was invited to Palestine as the guest of the Haganah.

Feivel Polkes informed Eichmann:

"Jewish nationalist circles were very pleased with the radical German policy, since the strength of the Jewish population in Palestine would be so far increased thereby that in the foreseeable future the Jews could reckon upon numerical superiority over the Arabs."[83]

The list of acts of Zionist collaboration with the Nazis goes on and on. What can account for this incredible willingness of Zionist leaders to betray the Jews of Europe? The entire rationale for the state of Israel offered by its apologists has been that it was intended to be the refuge of Jews facing persecution.

The Zionists, to the contrary, saw any effort to rescue Europe's Jews not as the fulfillment of their political purpose but as a threat to their entire movement. If Europe's Jews were saved, they would

50   *The Hidden History of Zionism*

wish to go elsewhere and the rescue operation would have nothing to do with the Zionist project of conquering Palestine.

Sacrificing Europe's Jews

The correlative to the acts of collaboration with the Nazis throughout the 1930's was that when attempts to change the immigration laws of the United States and Western Europe were contemplated in order to provide token refuge for persecuted Jews of Europe, it was the Zionists who actively organized to stop these efforts.

Ben Gurion informed a meeting of Labor Zionists in Great Britain in 1938: "If I knew that it would be possible to save all the children in Germany by bringing them over to England and only half of them by transporting them to Eretz Israel, then I opt for the second alternative."[84]

This obsession with colonizing Palestine and overwhelming the Arabs led the Zionist movement to oppose any rescue of the Jews facing extermination, because the ability to deflect select manpower to Palestine would be impeded. From 1933 to 1935, the WZO turned down two-thirds of all the German Jews who applied for immigration certificates.

Berel Katznelson, editor of the Labor Zionist *Davar,* described the "cruel criteria of Zionism:" German Jews were too old to bear children in Palestine, lacked trades for building a Zionist colony, didn't speak Hebrew and weren't Zionists. In place of these Jews facing extermination the WZO brought to Palestine 6,000 trained young Zionists from the United States, Britain and other safe countries. Worse than this, the WZO not merely failed to seek any alternative for the Jews facing the Holocaust, the Zionist leadership opposed belligerently all efforts to find refuge for fleeing Jews.

As late as 1943, while the Jews of Europe were being exterminated in their millions, the U.S. Congress proposed to set up a commission to "study" the problem. Rabbi Stephen Wise, who was the principal American spokesperson for Zionism, came to Washington to testify against the rescue bill because it would divert attention from the colonization of Palestine.

This is the same Rabbi Wise who, in 1938, in his capacity as leader of the American Jewish Congress, wrote a letter in which he opposed any change in U.S. immigration laws which would enable Jews to find refuge. He stated:

"It may interest you to know that some weeks ago the representatives of all the leading Jewish organizations met in conference. ... It was decided that no Jewish organization would, at this time, sponsor a bill which would in any way alter the immigration laws."[85]

Fighting Asylum

The entire Zionist establishment made its position unmistakable in its response to a motion by 227 British members of Parliament calling on the government to provide asylum in British territories for persecuted Jews. The meager undertaking which was prepared was as follows:

"His Majesty's Government issued some hundreds of Mauritius and other immigration permits in favor of threatened Jewish families."[86]

But even this token measure was opposed by the Zionist leaders. At a Parliamentary meeting on January 27, 1943, when the next steps were being pursued by over one hundred members of Parliament, a spokesperson for the Zionists announced that they opposed this motion because it did not contain preparations for the colonization of Palestine. This was a consistent stance.

Chaim Weizmann, the Zionist leader who had arranged the Balfour Declaration and was to become the first president of Israel, made this Zionist policy very explicit:

"The hopes of Europe's six million Jews are centered on emigration. I was asked: 'Can you bring six million Jews to Palestine?' I replied, 'No.' ... From the depths of the tragedy I want to save ... young people [for Palestine]. The old ones will pass. They will bear their fate or they will not. They are dust, economic and moral dust in a cruel world. ... Only the branch of the young shall survive. They have to accept it."[87]

Yitzhak Gruenbaum, the chairperson of the committee set up by the Zionists, nominally to investigate the condition of European Jews, said:

"When they come to us with two plans—the rescue of the masses of Jews in Europe or the redemption of the land—I vote, without a second thought, for the redemption of the land. The more said about the slaughter of our people, the greater the minimization of our efforts to strengthen and promote the Hebraisation of the land. If there would be a possibility today of buying packages of food with the money of the Karen Hayesod [United Jewish Appeal] to send it through Lisbon, would we do such a thing? No. And once again no!"[88]

Betraying the Resistance

In July 1944, the Slovakian Jewish leader Rabbi Dov Michael Weissmandel in a letter to Zionist officials charged with these "rescue organizations," proposed a series of measures to save the Jews scheduled for liquidation at Auschwitz. He offered exact mappings of the railways and urged the bombing of the tracks on which the Hungarian Jews were being transported to the crematoria.

He appealed for the bombing of the furnaces at Auschwitz, for the parachuting of ammunition to 80,000 prisoners, for the parachuting of saboteurs to blow up all the means of annihilation and thus end the cremation of 13,000 Jews *every day*.

Should the Allies refuse the organized and public demand by the "rescue organizations," Weissmandel proposed that the Zionists, who had funds and organization, obtain airplanes, recruit Jewish volunteers and carry out the sabotage.

Weissmandel was not alone. Throughout the late thirties and forties, Jewish spokespersons in Europe cried out for help, for public campaigns, for organized resistance, for demonstrations to force the hand of allied Governments—only to be met not merely by Zionist silence but by active Zionist sabotage of the meager efforts which were proposed or prepared in Great Britain and the United States.

Here is the *cri-de-coeur* of Rabbi Weissmandel. Writing to the Zionists in July 1944 he asked incredulously:

"Why have you done nothing until now? Who is guilty of this frightful negligence? Are you not guilty, our Jewish brothers: you who have the greatest good fortune in the world—liberty?"

"We send you," Rabbi Weissmandel wrote again—"this special message: to inform you that yesterday the Germans began the deportation of Jews from Hungary. ... The deported ones go to Auschwitz to be put to death by cyanide gas. This is the schedule of Auschwitz from yesterday to the end:

"Twelve thousand Jews—men, women and children, old men, infants, healthy and sick ones, are to be suffocated daily.

"And you, our brothers in Palestine, in all the countries of freedom, and you ministers of all the Kingdoms, how do you keep silent in the face of this great murder?

"Silent while thousands upon thousands, reaching now to six million Jews, are murdered? And silent now, while tens of thousands are still being murdered and waiting to be murdered? Their destroyed hearts cry out to you for help as they bewail your cruelty.

"Brutal, you are and murderers, too, you are, because of the cold-bloodedness of the silence in which you watch, because you sit with folded arms and do nothing, although you could stop or delay the murder of Jews at this very hour.

"You, our brothers, sons of Israel, are you insane? Don't you know the hell around us? For whom are you saving your money? Murderers! Madmen! Who is it that gives charity: you who toss a few pennies from your safe homes, or we who give our blood in the depths of hell?"[90]

No Zionist leader supported his request, nor did the Western capitalist regimes bomb a single concentration camp.

A Pact Against Hungary's Jews

The culmination of Zionist betrayal was the sacrifice of Hungary's Jews in a series of agreements between the Zionist movement and Nazi Germany which first became known in 1953. Dr. Rudolph Kastner of the Jewish Agency Rescue Committee in Budapest signed a secret pact with Adolf Eichmann to "settle the Jewish question" in Hungary. This took place in 1944. The pact sealed the fate of 800,000 Jews.

It was to be revealed later that Kastner was under the direction of the Zionist leaders abroad when he made his agreement with Eichmann. The agreement entailed the saving of six hundred prominent Jews on the condition that silence was maintained about the fate of Hungarian Jewry.

When a survivor, Malchiel Greenwald, exposed the pact and denounced Kastner as a Nazi collaborator whose "deeds in Budapest cost the lives of hundreds of thousands of Jews,"[91] Greenwald was sued by the Israeli government, whose leaders had drawn up the terms of the Kastner pact.

The Israeli Court came to the following conclusion:

"The sacrifice of the majority of the Jews, in order to rescue the prominents was the basic element in the agreement between Kastner and the Nazis. This agreement fixed the division of the nation into two unequal camps, a small fragment of prominents, whom the Nazis promised Kastner to save, on the one hand, and the great majority of Hungarian Jews whom the Nazis designated for death, on the other hand."⁹²

The court declared that the imperative condition of this pact was that neither Kastner nor the Zionist leaders would interfere in the action of the Nazis against the Jews. These leaders undertook not only to eschew interference, but they agreed they would not, in the words of the Israeli court, "hamper them in the extermination."

"Collaboration between the Jewish Agency Rescue Committee and the exterminators of the Jews was solidified in Budapest and Vienna. Kastner's duties were part and parcel of the S.S. In addition to its Extermination Department and Looting Department, the Nazi S.S. opened a Rescue Department headed by Kastner."⁹³

Saving Nazis, Not Jews

It is not surprising that it was to be revealed that Kastner intervened to save S.S. General Kurt Becher from being tried for war crimes. Becher was one of the leading negotiators of the deal with the Zionists in 1944. He was also an S.S. Major in Poland, a member of the Death Corps "that worked around the clock killing Jews." "Becher distinguished himself as a Jew slaughterer in Poland and Russia."⁹⁴

He was appointed Commissar of all Nazi concentration camps by Heinrich Himmler.

What happened to him? He became president of many corporations and headed up the sale of wheat to Israel. His corporation, the Cologne-Handel Gesselschaft, did extensive business with the Israeli government.

A Military Pact with Nazism

On January 11, 1941, Avraham Stern proposed a formal military pact between the National Military Organization (NMO), of which Yitzhak Shamir, the current Prime Minister of Israel, was a prominent leader, and the Nazi Third Reich. This proposal became known as the Ankara document, having been discovered after the war in the files of the German Embassy in Turkey. It states the following:

"The evacuation of the Jewish masses from Europe is a precondition for solving the Jewish question; but this can only be made possible and complete through the settlement of these masses in the home of the Jewish people, Palestine, and through the establishment of a Jewish state in its historical boundaries. ...

"The NMO, which is well-acquainted with the goodwill of the

German Reich government and its authorities towards Zionist activity inside Germany and towards Zionist emigration plans, is of the opinion that:

"1. Common interests could exist between the establishment of a New Order in Europe in conformity with the German concept, and the true national aspirations of the Jewish people as they are embodied by the NMO.

"2. Cooperation between the new Germany and renewed folkish-national Hebraium would be possible and

"3. The establishment of the historical Jewish state on a national and totalitarian basis, and bound by a treaty with the German Reich, would be in the interest of a maintained and strengthened future German position of power in the Near East.

"Proceeding from these considerations, the NMO in Palestine, under the condition that the above-mentioned national aspirations of the Israeli freedom movement are recognized on the side of the German Reich, offers to actively take part in the war on Germany's side."[95]

Zionism's Perfidy

Zionism's perfidy—the betrayal of the victims of the Holocaust—was the culmination of their attempt to identify the interests of the Jews with those of the established order. Today, the Zionists join their state to the enforcement arm of U.S. imperialism—from the death squads of Latin America to the covert operations of the C.I.A. on four continents.

This sordid history is rooted in the demoralization of the founders of Zionism, who rejected the possibility of overcoming anti-Semitism through popular struggle and social revolution. Moses Hess, Theodor Herzl and Chaim Weizmann chose the wrong side of the barricades—that of state power, class domination and exploitative rule. They propounded a putative disjunction between emancipation from persecution and the necessity of social change. They fully understood that the cultivation of anti-Semitism and the persecution of the Jews were the work of the very ruling class from whom they curried favor.

In seeking the sponsorship of the anti-Semites themselves, they revealed several motives: the worship of power with which they associated strength; a desire to end Jewish "weakness" and vulnerability, ceasing to be perpetual outsiders.

This sensibility was a short step to assimilating the values and ideas of the Jew-haters themselves. The Jews, the Zionists wrote, were indeed an undisciplined, subversive, dissident people, worthy of the scorn they had earned. The Zionists catered shamelessly to racist Jew-hatred. Worshipping power, they appealed to the anti-Semitic desire of the Von Plehves and the Himmlers to be rid of a victim people long radicalized by persecution, a people who filled the ranks of revolutionary movements and whose suffering drew their best minds to intellectual ferment offensive to established values.

The dirty secret of Zionist history is that Zionism was threatened by the Jews themselves. Defending the Jewish people from persecution meant organizing resistance to the regimes which menaced them. But these regimes embodied the imperial order which comprised the only social force willing or able to impose a settler colony on the Palestinian people. Hence, the Zionists needed the persecution of the Jews to persuade Jews to become colonizers afar, and they needed the persecutors to sponsor the enterprise.

But European Jewry had never manifested any interest in colonizing Palestine. Zionism remained a fringe movement among the Jews, who aspired to live in the countries of their birth free of discrimination or to escape persecution by emigrating to bourgeois democracies perceived as more tolerant.

Zionism, therefore, could never answer the needs or aspirations of the Jews. The moment of truth came when persecution gave way to physical extermination. Put to the ultimate and sole test of their real relationship to Jewish survival, the Zionists did not merely fail to lead resistance or defend the Jews, they actively sabotaged Jewish efforts to boycott the Nazi economy. They sought, even then, the sponsorship of the mass murderers themselves, not merely because the Third Reich appeared powerful enough to impose a Zionist colony, but because the Nazi practices were *consonant* with Zionist assumptions.

There was a common ground between the Nazis and the Zionists, expressed not merely in the proposal of Shamir's National Military Organization to form a state in Palestine on a "national totalitarian basis."

Vladimir Jabotinsky, in his last work, "The Jewish War Front," (1940) wrote of his plans for the Palestinian people:

"Since we have this great moral authority for calmly envisaging the exodus of Arabs, we need not regard the possible departure of 900,000 with dismay. Herr Hitler has recently been enhancing the popularity of population transfer."[96]

Jabotinsky's remarkable declaration in "The Jewish War Front" synthesizes Zionist thought and its moral bankruptcy. The slaughter of the Jews gave Zionism "great moral authority"—For what? "For calmly envisaging the exodus of *Arabs*." The lesson of Nazi destruction of the Jews was that it was permissible now for Zionists to visit the same fate upon the entire Palestinian population.

Seven years later, the Zionists emulated the Nazis, whose backing they sought and even at times achieved, and they covered bleeding Palestine in multiple Lidices,[97] driving 800,000 people into exile.

The Zionists approached the Nazis in the same spirit they had Von Plehve, acting on the perverse notion that Jew-hatred was useful. Their purpose was not rescue, but forced conscription of the select few—the rest to be consigned to their agonizing fate.

Zionism sought bodies with which to colonize Palestine and preferred Jewish corpses in their millions to any rescue that might settle Jews elsewhere.

If ever a people could be expected to grasp the meaning of persecution, the pain of being perpetual refugees and the humiliation of slander, it ought to have been the Jews.

In place of compassion, the Zionists celebrated the persecution of others, even as they first betrayed the Jews and then degraded them. They selected a victim people of their own on whom to inflict a conquering design. They aligned the surviving Jews with a new genocide against the Palestinian people, cloaking themselves, with savage irony, in the collective shroud of the Holocaust.

CHAPTER SEVEN

The Myth of Security

"Security" has been the catch-phrase deployed to screen widespread massacre of civilian populations throughout Palestine and Lebanon, for the confiscation of Palestinian and Arab land, for the expansion into surrounding territory and the establishment of new settlements, for deportation and for sustained torture of political prisoners.

The publication of the "Personal Diary of Moshe Sharett" ("Yoman ishi, Maariv," Tel Aviv, 1979) demolished the myth of security as the motor force of Israeli policy. Moshe Sharett was a former Prime Minister of Israel (1954-55), director of the Jewish Agency's Political Department and Foreign Minister (1948-56).

Sharett's diary reveals in explicit language that the Israeli political and military leadership never believed in any Arab danger to Israel. They sought to maneuver and force the Arab states into military confrontations which the Zionist leadership were certain of winning so Israel could carry out the destabilization of Arab regimes and the planned occupation of additional territory.

Sharett described the governing motive of Israeli military provocation:

"To bring about the liquidation of all ... Palestinian claims to Palestine through the dispersion of the Palestinian refugees to distant corners of the world."[98]

The Sharett diaries document a longstanding program of Israel's leaders from both Labor and Likud: to "dismember the Arab world, defeat the Arab national movement and create puppet regimes under regional Israeli power."[99]

Sharett cites cabinet meetings, position papers and policy memoranda which prepared wars "to modify the balance of power in the region radically, transforming Israel into the major power in the Middle East."[100]

Sharett reveals that far from Israel "reacting" to Nasser's nationalization of the Suez Canal for its war of October 1956, the Israeli leadership had prepared this war and had it on their agenda from autumn 1953, one year before Nasser came to power. Sharett recounts how the Israeli cabinet had agreed that international conditions for this war would mature within three years. The explicit intent was "the absorption of the Gaza territory and of the Sinai."

A timetable for conquest was decided at the highest military and political level. The occupation of Gaza and the West Bank was prepared in the early 1950's. In 1954, David Ben Gurion and Moshe Dayan developed a detailed plan to instigate internal Lebanese conflict in order to fragment Lebanon. This was sixteen years before an organized Palestinian political presence occurred there in the aftermath of the expulsions from Jordan in 1970, when King Hussein slaughtered Palestinians in what came to be known as "Black September."

Sharett described "the use of terror and aggression to provoke" in order to facilitate conquest:

"I have been meditating on the long chain of false incidents and hostilities we have invented and on the many clashes we have provoked which cost so much blood, and on the violations of law by our men— all of which have brought grave disaster and determined the whole course of events."[101]

Sharett recounts how on October 11, 1953, Israeli President Ben Zvi "raised as usual some inspired questions such as [our] chance to occupy the Sinai and how wonderful it would be if the Egyptians started an offensive so we could follow with an invasion of the desert."[102]

On October 26, 1953, Sharett writes:

"1) The Army considers the present border with Jordan as absolutely unacceptable. 2) The Army is planning war in order to occupy the rest of Eretz Israel."[103]

By January 31, 1954, Dayan outlined war plans, disclosed by Sharett:

"We should advance militarily into Syria and realize a series of faits accomplis. The interesting conclusion from all this regards the direction in which the Chief of Staff is thinking."[104]

Absorbing Lebanon

In May 1954, Ben Gurion and Dayan formulated a war plan for the absorption of Lebanon:

"According to Dayan, the only thing that's necessary is to find an officer, even just a Major. We should ... buy him ... to make him agree to declare himself the savior of the Maronite population.

"Then the Israeli army will enter Lebanon, will occupy the necessary territory and will create a Christian regime which will ally itself with Israel. The territory from the Litani southward will be totally annexed to Israel and everything will be all right.

"If we were to accept the advice of the Chief of Staff we would do it tomorrow, without awaiting a signal [sic] from Baghdad."[105]

But twelve days later, Dayan had moved into high gear for the planned invasion, occupation and dismemberment of Lebanon:

"The Chief of Staff supports a plan to hire a Lebanese officer who will agree to serve as a puppet so that the Israeli army may appear as responding to his appeal 'to liberate Lebanon from its Muslim oppressors.'"[106]

The entire scenario, therefore, for the 1982 war in Lebanon was in place twenty-eight years earlier, before the P.L.O. existed.

Sharett, who opposed the original action, recounts how the invasion of Lebanon was postponed.

Green Light from the C.I.A.

"The C.I.A. gave Israel the 'green light' to attack Egypt. The energies of Israel's security establishment became wholly absorbed by the preparations for the war which would take place exactly one year later."[107]

The real relationship of Israel to the Arab national movement is placed by Sharett in the clear context of service to U.S. global dominion, of which Zionist expansion is an essential component:

"...We have a free hand and God bless us if we act audaciously. ... Now ... the U.S. is interested in toppling Nasser's regime ... but it does not dare at the moment to use the methods it adopted to topple the leftist government of Jacobo Arbenz in Guatemala [1954] and of Mossadegh in Iran [1953]. ... It prefers its work to be done by Israel.

"...Isser [General] proposes seriously and pressingly ... that we carry out our plan for the occupation of the Gaza Strip now. ... The situation is changed and there are other reasons which determine that it is 'time to act.' First the discovery of oil near the Strip ... its defense requires dominating the Strip—this alone is worth dealing with the troublesome question of the refugees."[108]

Moshe Sharett anticipated another wave of slaughter, which did, in fact, occur. On February 17, 1955, he wrote:

"...We cry out over our isolation and the dangers to our security, we initiate aggression and reveal ourselves as being bloodthirsty and aspiring to perpetrate mass massacres."[109]

Ben Gurion and Dayan proposed that Israel create a pretext to seize the Gaza Strip. Sharett's own evaluation on March 27, 1955, was prophetic:

"Let us assume that there are 200,000 Arabs in the Gaza Strip. Let us assume that half of them will run or will be made to run to the Hebron Hills. Obviously, they will run away without anything and shortly after they establish themselves in some stable environment, they will become again riotous and homeless. It is easy to imagine the outrage and hate and bitterness.

"...And we shall have 100,000 of them in the Strip, and it is easy to imagine what means we shall resort to in order to supress them and what kind of headlines we shall receive in the international press. The first round would be: Israel aggressively invades the Gaza Strip. The second: Israel causes again the terrified flight of masses of Arab refugees. Their hate will be rekindled by the atrocities that we shall cause them to suffer during the occupation."[110]

One year later, Dayan's troops occupied the Gaza Strip, Sinai, the Straits of Tiran and were deployed along the Suez Canal.

From Herzl to Dayan

The plans exposed by Moshe Sharett did not originate with David Ben Gurion or Moshe Dayan. In 1904, Theodor Herzl described the territory over which the Zionist movement laid claim as inclusive of all the land "from the Brook of Egypt to the Euphrates."[111]

The territory embraced all of Lebanon and Jordan, two thirds of Syria, one-half of Iraq, a strip of Turkey, one-half of Kuwait, one third of Saudi Arabia, the Sinai and Egypt, including Port Saïd, Alexandria and Cairo.

In his testimony before the United Nations Special Committee of Enquiry which was preparing the Partition of Palestine (July 9, 1947), Rabbi Fischmann, the official representative of the Jewish agency for Palestine, reiterated Herzl's claims:

"The Promised Land extends from the River of Egypt up to the Euphrates. It includes parts of Syria and Lebanon."[112]

CHAPTER EIGHT

Blitzkrieg and Slaughter

Zionist designs upon Lebanon long antedated the formation of the state of Israel. In 1918, Britain was informed of Zionist claims to Lebanon up to and inclusive of the Litani River. British plans in 1920 to designate the Litani the northern border of a Jewish state were altered in response to French objections.

By 1936, the Zionists had offered to support Maronite hegemony in Lebanon. The Maronite Patriarch then testified to the Peel Commission in favor of a Zionist state in Palestine. In 1937, Ben Gurion spoke of Zionist plans for Lebanon to the Zionist World Workers Party, which was meeting in Zurich:

"They are the natural ally of the land of Israel. The proximity of Lebanon will further our loyal allies as soon as the Jewish state is created and give us the possibility to expand...."[113]

In 1948, Israel occupied up to the Litani but withdrew a year later under pressure. Sharett reports of Ben Gurion's timetable in 1954 to induce the Maronites to fragment Lebanon:

"This is now the Central Task. ... We must invest the time and energy to bring about a fundamental change in Lebanon. Dollars should not be spared. ... We will not be forgiven if we miss the historic opportunity."[114]

The invasion of Lebanon in 1982 followed a series of raids and invasions in 1968, 1976, 1978 and 1981. Plans to dismember Lebanon were joined now to the primary objective of dispersing the Palestinian inhabitants of Lebanon through massacre followed by expulsion.

The invasion was planned jointly with the U.S. government. The Maronite Phalange was part of the project: "When Amin Gemayel visited Washington the previous Fall, he was asked by an American official when the invasion was due."[115]

Later, when Defense Minister Ariel Sharon visited Washington: "Secretary of State, Alexander Haig, gave the green light for the invasion."[116]

The invasion of Lebanon was launched under the rubric "Peace in the Galilee." Cruel irony! The original inhabitants of the Galilee had lived there for a millenium and were driven out by massacre in 1948.

They had settled near Sidon, setting up tents in a refugee camp they called Ain El Helweh, "Sweet Spring."

The camp was organized in areas corresponding to the Galilean communities from which people had come. A miniature Galilee, its areas replicated the villages of the homeland in the Diaspora tent town which was Ain El Helweh.

In 1952, they were allowed to convert tents into permanent structures and they numbered now, some 80,000, the largest Palestinian camp in Lebanon.

On Sunday, June 6, 1982, at 5:30 a.m., intensive aerial bombardment began with the onset of the invasion. The Israelis took Ain El Helweh as a grid, using a saturation-bombing pattern in a series of quadrants. First one quadrant was subjected to carpet bombing and then the next—methodically and relentlessly, the bombing of each quadrant renewed as the last was levelled. The bombing continued in this manner for ten days and nights. Cluster bombs, concussion bombs, high flaring incendiary bombs and white phosphorus were used.

It was followed by a further ten days of bombardment from the sea and air. Then bulldozers were brought by the Israelis to reduce to rubble what remained standing. Shelters were covered, burying people alive, their frantic family members clutching at the bulldozers. Norwegian health workers who survived, reported:

"It smelled like dead bodies everywhere. Everything was devastated."[117]

From 500,000 to 50,000

The invasion of Lebanon in the summer of 1982 had as its purpose the scattering through massacre and terror of the entire Palestinian population.

Prior to the invasion of Lebanon in 1982, Ariel Sharon and Bashir Gemayel had declared on separate occasions that they would reduce the Palestinians in Lebanon from 500,000 to 50,000. As the invasion unfolded, these plans began to surface in the pages of the Israeli and Western press. *Ha'aretz* reported on September 26, 1982:

"A long-term objective aimed at the expulsion of the whole Palestinian population of Lebanon beginning with Beirut. The purpose was to create a panic to convince [sic] all the Palestinians of Lebanon that they were no longer safe in that country."

The London *Sunday Times* reported on the same day:

"This carefully preplanned military operation to 'purge' the camps was called *Moah Barzel* or Iron Brain; the plan was familiar to Sharon and Begin and part of Sharon's larger plan discussed by the Israeli Cabinet on July 17."

Bashir Gemayel became emboldened as the Israeli blitzkrieg swept through Lebanon. "The Palestinians," he declared, "are a people too many. We will not rest until every true Lebanese has killed at least one Palestinian."[118]

A prominent Lebanese army doctor told his unit: "Soon there will not be a single Palestinian in Lebanon. They are a bacteria which must be exterminated."[119]

The Sabra and Shatila Massacres

The massacres which ensued bore a grim resemblance to the slaughter of the innocents engulfing Deir Yasin, Dueima, Kibya and Kfar Qasim as Palestine was depopulated from 1947 through the 1950's.

The Western and Israeli reports made the murderous purpose of Israel's invasion unmistakable:

"By Sharon's admission, the Israelis planned two weeks ago to have the Lebanese Forces enter the camps," wrote *Time Magazine*. Later in the same article, it became clear that this had been prepared long before:

"Top Israeli officers planned many months ago to enlist the Lebanese Forces, made up of the combined Christian militias headed by Bashir Gemayel, to enter the Palestinian refugee camps once an Israeli encirclement of West Beirut had been completed.

"On several occasions Gemayal told Israeli officials he would raze the camps and flatten them into tennis courts. This fits in with Israeli thinking. The Christian militia forces that were known to have gone into the camps were trained by the Israelis."[120]

The Israeli press was equally explicit in its reports of Israeli plans. On September 15, *Ha'aretz* quoted Chief of Staff General Raphael Eitan: "All four Palestinian camps are surrounded and hermetically sealed."

The New York Times had corroborated the *Time Magazine* account:

"Sharon told the Knesset that the General Staff and the Commander in Chief of the Phalangists met twice with Israel's ranking generals on September 15 and discussed entering the camps which they did the next afternoon."[121]

The Killer Militia

Two months before the massacre of Sabra and Shatila, perhaps the most remarkable account appeared in the *Jerusalem Post*. A long interview was published with Major Etienne Saqr [code name, Abu Arz]. Major Saqr was the leader of the several-thousand-strong right-wing militia, "The Guardians of the Cedars."

The *Jerusalem Post* disclosed that Major Saqr "is about to leave for the United States to put his credo and solutions" before Americans. "Since 1975, he has propagated the Israeli solution ... and Israel has supported him in every possible material way."[122]

Major Saqr's own remarks foreshadowed what would later shock the world at the Palestinian camps of Sabra and Shatila:

"It is the Palestinians we have to deal with. Ten years ago there were 84,000; now there are between 600,000 and 700,000. In six years there will be two million. We can't let it come to that."

When asked by the *Jerusalem Post*: "What is your solution?" Major Saqr replied: "Very simple. We shall drive them to the borders of 'brotherly' Syria. ... Anyone who looks back, stops or returns will be shot on the spot. We have the moral right, reinforced by well-organized public relations plans and political preparations."

"Are you," asked the *Jerusalem Post*, "able to implement this threat? (He does not blink an eyelid.) 'Of course we can. And we shall.'"

Major Saqr had played a major role in the 1976 massacre of Palestinians in Tal al Zaatar refugee camp.

After the massacres of Sabra and Shatila, Major Saqr returned to Jerusalem to hold a press conference in which he took responsibility for carrying out the massacre with the Israelis: "No one has the right to criticize us; we carried out our duty, our sacred responsibility."[123]

He left this press conference where he claimed a share in the "credit" for mass murder to attend a meeting with Prime Minister Menachem Begin.

Major Saqr surfaced again, now based in the Israeli command headquarters in the Suraya complex in Sidon, near Ain El Helweh. His militia distributed leaflets throughout Sidon which read:

"Germs live only in rot. Let us prevent rot from infiltrating society. Let us continue the work of destruction of the last bastions of the Palestinians and smash whatever life is left in this poisonous snake."

Major Saqr had worked closely with the notorious intelligence chief for Bashir Gemayel's militia, Elie Hobeika. Hobeika was known as the

C.I.A.'s man in Beirut.

Jonathan Randal of the *Washington Post* cited Hobeika's declarations in Beirut, ascribing these to "one of the killers;" they echoed those of Major Saqr in Jerusalem:

"Shoot them against the pink and blue walls; slaughter them in the half-light of the evening. The only way you will find out how many Palestinians we killed is if they ever build a subway under Beirut. ... A good massacre or two will drive the Palestinians out of Beirut and Lebanon once and for all."[124]

The Israeli Army command had also enlisted leading Lebanese officers. One of them revealed:

"During Thursday, General Drori, took me to the airport where Israelis were assembling the militia. 'If your men won't do it, I know others who will.'"[125]

He referred to Saqr: "...The Guardians of the Cedars, whom Gemayel incorporated into the Lebanese Forces in 1980, held, as an article of faith, that Palestinian infants must be killed since they eventually grew up to be terrorists."[126]

Each Of You Is An Avenger

The brutality of the invasion and occupation of Lebanon and the chilling horror of the massacres in Sabra and Shatila once again removed the mask from the cruel face of Zionism. Television and newspaper coverage of the war produced a world-wide outcry, forcing Israel to dissimulate and to appoint an official Commission of Inquiry. The Israeli government conducted its own investigation under the Kahan Commission.

The "investigation" concluded, predictably, that the Israelis were merely negligent in underestimating "Arab blood lust," but had no direct role in the massacre of Sabra and Shatila.

The German weekly *Der Spiegel*, however, carried an interview on February 14, 1983, with one of the killer militia, who recounted not only his own role in the slaughter, but described direct Israeli participation.

The article was entitled "Each Of You Is An Avenger," and the first person account could have come from the Nuremberg Trials:

"We met in the Schahrur Wadi, in the valley of the nightingales Southeast of Beirut. It was Wednesday, the fifteenth of September. ... We were approximately three hundred men from East Beirut, South

Lebanon and the Akkar Mountains in the north. ... I belonged to the Tiger Militia of ex-President Camile Chamoun.

"Phalange officers summoned us and brought us to the meeting place. They told us that they needed us for a 'special action.'...You are the agents of good, the officers told us repeatedly. 'Each of you is an avenger.'...

"Then a good dozen Israelis in green uniforms without indication of rank came along. They had playing cards with them and spoke Arabic well, except that like all Jews they pronounced the hard 'h' as 'ch.' They were talking about the Palestinian camps Sabra and Shatila ... it was clear to us what we were to do, and we were looking forward to it.

"We had to swear an oath never to divulge anything about our action. At about 10 p.m. we climbed into an American army truck that the Israelis had given over to us. We parked the vehicle near the airport tower. There, immediately next to the Israeli positions, several such trucks were already parked.

"Some Israelis in Phalange uniforms were with the Party. 'The Israeli friends who accompany you,' our officers told us '...will make your work easier.' They directed us not to make use of our firearms, if at all possible. 'Everything must proceed noiselessly.' ... We saw other comrades. They had to do their work with bayonets and knives. Bloody corpses were lying in the alleys. The half-asleep women and children who cried out for help put our whole plan in danger, alarming the entire camp.

"Now I saw once again the Israelis who had been at our secret meeting. One signalled us to move back to areas of the camp entrance. The Israelis opened up with all their guns. The Israelis helped us with floodlights.

"There were shocking scenes that showed what the Palestinians were good for. A few, including women, had taken shelter in a small alley, behind some donkeys. Unfortunately we had to shoot down these poor animals to finish off the Palestinians behind them. It got to me when the animals cried out in pain. It was gruesome.

"A comrade entered a house full of women and children. The Palestinians screamed and threw their gas stoves on the ground. We sent the hard-hearted rabble to hell.

"At about four in the morning my squad went back to the truck. When there was morning light we went back into the camp. We went past bodies, stumbled over bodies, shot and stabbed all eyewitnesses.

Killing others was easy once you have done it a few times.

"Now came the Israeli Army bulldozers. 'Plow everything under the ground. Don't let any witnesses stay alive.' But despite our efforts, the area was still teeming with people. They ran about and caused awful confusion. The order to 'plow them under' demanded too much.

"It became clear that the pretty plan had failed. Thousands had escaped us. Far too many Palestinians are still alive. Everywhere now people are talking about a massacre and feeling sorry for the Palestinians. Who appreciates the hardships that we took upon ourselves. ... Just think. I fought for twenty-four hours in Shatila without food or drink."

The death toll in Sabra and Shatila was over 3,000. Many of the mass graves were never opened.

Destroying Lebanon

The slaughter and dispersal of the Palestinian people was one component of Israeli strategy. Another was the decimation of the vital Lebanese economy which, despite Israeli efforts, had emerged as the finance capital of the Middle East.

Twenty thousand Palestinians and Lebanese died, 25,000 were wounded and 400,000 were made homeless during the first months of the 1982 Israeli invasion. The tonnages dropped on Beirut alone surpassed those of the atomic bomb which devastated Hiroshima. Schools and hospitals were particularly targeted.

Virtually all rolling stock and heavy equipment from Lebanese factories were looted and taken to Israel. Even the lathes and smaller machine tools from the U.N.R.W.A. vocational training centers were pillaged.

The citrus and olive production of Lebanon south of Beirut was destroyed. The Lebanese economy, whose exports had competed with Israel's, became moribund. The south of Lebanon became an Israeli market even as the headwaters of the Litani River, like the Jordan River before it, were diverted by the Israelis.

The author of this book experienced the bombing and siege of West Beirut in 1982, lived with Palestinians in the ruins of Ain El Helweh during Israeli occupation and witnessed the devastation in the Palestinian camps of Rashidya, El Bas, Burj al Jamali, Mieh Mieh, Burj al Burajneh, Sabra and Shatila, as well as the destruction of the Lebanese towns and villages throughout the south.

The accounts of Israeli enactment of the massacre of Sabra and Shatila have been substantiated by this author, who was present in the camps on the final day of slaughter. He and Mya Shone photographed Israeli tanks and soldiers in Sabra and Shatila and spoke to the survivors over a period of four days.

CHAPTER NINE

The Second Occupation

Menachem Begin, Ariel Sharon and Shimon Peres have, at different times, expressed the conviction that "the lesson of Lebanon" would pacify, by example, the Palestinians of the West Bank and the Gaza Strip.

This pacification, however, had been underway for twenty-one years since their occupation in 1967. Many in the West Bank and Gaza were refugees of earlier Israeli depredations from 1947 to 1967.

In the post-1967 territories of occupation, a Palestinian cannot plant a tomato without an unobtainable permit from the military government. He or she cannot plant an eggplant without such a permit. You cannot whitewash your house. You can't fix a pane of glass. You can't sink a well. You can't wear a shirt which has the colors of the Palestinian flag. You can't have a cassette in your house which has Palestinian national songs.

Since 1967, more than 300,000 Palestinian youth have passed through Israeli prisons under conditions of institutional torture. Amnesty International concluded that there is no country in the world in which the use of official and sustained torture is as well-established and documented as in the case of the state of Israel.

Twenty-one years after the Israeli seizure of Gaza, the *Los Angeles Times* described its consequences:

"Only about 2,200 Jewish settlers live in the Gaza Strip, which was captured from Egypt, but they occupy about 30% of the 135 square mile area. More than 650,000 Palestinians, mostly refugees, are squeezed into about half the strip, making it one of the most densely populated areas in the world. The rest of Gaza's land has been designated restricted border zones by the army."[127]

Civil Rights and the Law

Arrest:

In all territory under Israeli military occupation, any soldier or policeman has the right to detain an individual should he believe he has "grounds to suspect" that the person in question has committed an offense. The law does not set out the nature of the infraction suspected by the soldier to have been committed or planned.[128]

The deliberately vague nature of this statute has the consequence of denying to Palestinians in the territories occupied since 1967 any means of knowing why they may be arrested and detained.

Upon arrest for suspicion, a Palestinian may be detained for eighteen days with the approval of a police officer.

Once arrested, a Palestinian detainee can be (and virtually always is) denied access to a lawyer. The formal regulation provides that the Prison Administrator decide whether or not a lawyer may be permitted to see a client.

Routinely, prison officials rule that for a prisoner to meet with an attorney before interrogation is complete would be to "hinder the process of interrogation."[129] This decision can extend through the duration of detention. As a result, lawyers gain access to a prisoner only *after* that prisoner has confessed or after the security services have decided to terminate the interrogation.

Lawyers in Israel maintain that the reason for this arrangement is that the focal point of interrogation is to obtain a confession. To achieve that end the authorities invariably subject a prisoner to isolation, torture and insupportable physical conditions.

Upon arrest, a detainee undergoes a period of starvation, deprivation of sleep by organized methods and prolonged periods during which the prisoner is made to stand with hands cuffed and raised, a filthy sack covering the head. Prisoners are dragged on the ground, beaten with objects, kicked, summarily stripped and placed under ice-cold showers. Verbal abuse and physical humiliation are commonplace involving such acts as spitting or urinating into a prisoner's mouth and forcing the prisoner to crawl around in a crowded cell.

The interrogation can go on for several *months* until such time as the individual confesses and a charge can thus be drawn up. If the prisoner does not break under torture and agree to confess, he or she may be detained administratively, without being charged or brought to trial.

Confessions:

The coerced confession is central to proceedings against Palestinian prisoners. Until 1981 a prisoner could be tried only on the basis of his or her personal confession—a sufficient inducement for prison authorities to produce one for the court. Wasfi O. Masri, who had been a senior judge under Jordanian rule and who defends many Palestinian prisoners has stated:

"In 90% of the cases I have, the prisoner ... was beaten and tortured."[130]

Because many prisoners withstood torture and refused to confess, an amendment to the military statute was adopted, permitting courts to use as the central and, indeed, sole evidence against a defendant the fact that his or her name was mentioned in someone else's confession.

While "evidence" is considered inculpating if a defendant's name is cited in another prisoner's confession, the prosecution's case is treated as definitive if a defendant's confession is produced. If a detainee fails to admit to an offense, officers of the Intelligence Services are brought into court to testify that the prisoner made an "oral" confession. Palestinian attorney Mohammed Na'amneh, in describing two such cases, observed that when prisoners deny having confessed orally, the court accepts an Intelligence Officer's testimony as probative.[131]

All confessions are written in Hebrew, a language virtually none of the Palestinians from the territories occupied since 1967 is able to read. When prisoners refuse to sign on the ground that they cannot read Hebrew, they are abused. In the case of Shehadeh Shalaldeh of Ramallah, "the officer left the room and two men in civilian clothes came in. I told them I wanted to know what I was signing. ... They started beating me, so I said, 'Okay, okay, I'll sign.'"[132]

There are many cases wherein the statement which a prisoner has signed in Hebrew bears no relation to the Arabic text originally shown him. Such confessions invariably begin:

"I was a member of a terrorist organization." These words would never be used by a member of the P.L.O. (Palestine Liberation Organization) or its component organizations. Notwithstanding the fact that such "confessions" are in a language which cannot be read by those signing them, the courts have ruled that confessions are "irreversible" and wholly probative of the offense in question.

Exact data on the percentage of those arrested, interrogated and eventually brought to trial are difficult to establish with precision. No published statistics exist. But the cumulative information of lawyers and Palestinian community records make evident that the number of Palestinians subjected to interrogation and torture is enormous.

Israeli lawyers state without hesitation that most males over the age of sixteen have been interrogated and held at one or another time in their lives for periods of varying duration. By 1980, reports printed in the Israeli press estimated the number of Palestinians imprisoned at one or another time after 1967 to have reached 200,000. Lawyers recently updated this figure to 300,000.

Trial:

Those who reach trial are charged most commonly with "political" offenses which include: 1) Breaking public order (a vague category embracing any action including insufficient subservience toward Israeli officials); 2) Demonstrating; 3) Distributing leaflets or daubing slogans; 4) Membership in an "illegal" organization. Specifically targeted are groups which attempt to form any Palestinian political party in pre-1967 Israel such as El Ard (The Land), which does not support explicitly a Jewish state, or representative Palestinian bodies, such as the National Guidance Committee (Lijni Komite al Watani) in the West Bank. Organizations which are part of the P.L.O. are also among those declared illegal.

Many youngsters in the Occupied Territories who strike, march, demonstrate or meet, are *charged* with "producing or throwing Molotov cocktails." A significant number of people are tried for possession of arms, armed assault and forms of military operation and sabotage. Many of these cases involve, in fact, violation of the "contact with the enemy" provision, which covers any organization designated by Israeli security forces as sympathetic to Palestinian national aspirations.

Within ten years of the occupation, over 60% of all prisoners in pre-1967 Israel and the territories occupied since 1967 were Palestinians found guilty of political offenses. All political offenses violate the Defense Emergency Regulations of 1945 and the State Security, Foreign Relations and Official Secrets Act of 1967, thus making them "security offenses."

People charged with such political offenses are brought to trial in military courts. This is true inside pre-1967 Israel as well as the territories occupied subsequently. Palestinians are rarely tried in civil court.

The Defense Emergency Regulations

Under the Emergency Regulations, a military commander (currently the Military Governor) can, at his discretion and without judicial review:
  - imprison people indefinitely

- prohibit travel within or outside pre-1967 Israel and the territories occupied since 1967
- expel an individual permanently
- restrict any person to his or her home, locality, village or town
- forbid anyone to make use of his or her own property
- order the demolition of homes
- impose police surveillance on any individual and order him or her to report to a police station several times a day
- declare any area closed as a security zone, whether it be a farm owned by a family, an inhabited village, refugee camp or tribal lands
- censor all media, requiring all articles, leaflets and books to be approved, and banning their distribution
- raid people's homes and confiscate entire libraries
- forbid the gathering of ten or more people for the purpose of discussing politics
- forbid membership in an organization.

Military edicts appended to the Defense Emergency Regulations have proliferated to the point where they impinge upon the minutiae of Palestinian existence. Military Orders affecting the West Bank:
- forbid the planting of tomatos or eggplant without written permission
- forbid the planting of any fruit tree without written permission
- forbid *any* repairs to a house or structure without written permission
- forbid the sinking of wells for drinking water or irrigation.

The Defense Emergency Regulations, first adopted by the British to control the Palestinian population within the Mandate, were revised in 1945 and used by the British to control armed attacks on British soldiers by the Irgun and Haganah and to restrict Zionist acquisition of land. The Regulations were condemned in 1946 by the Hebrew Lawyers Union in the following terms:

"The powers given to the ruling authority in the Emergency Regulations deny the inhabitants of Palestine their basic human rights. These regulations undermine the foundation of law and justice; they constitute a serious danger to individual freedom, and they institute a regime of arbitrariness without any judicial supervision."[133]

Yaakov Shimpshon Shapira, who was later to become a Minister of Justice for the state of Israel and one of its leading legal authorities, proclaimed:

"The regime built in Palestine on the Defense Emergency Regulations has no parallel in any civilized nation. Even in Nazi Germany there were no such laws and the Nazi deeds of Mayadink and other similar things were against the code of laws. Only in an occupied country do you find a system resembling ours...."[134]

Notwithstanding these assessments by leading Zionist authorities in jurisprudence, the Defense Emergency Regulations were incorporated into the legal system of the state of Israel. Since the founding of the state in 1948, the basic regulations have remained unchanged.

The irony is evident. The very regulations characterized by the man who would become Israel's Minister of Justice as "unparalleled in any civilized country" and condemned by Zionist lawyers for denying "basic human rights" were adopted as the law of the land. As Yaakov Shimshon Shapira stressed: "Only in an occupied country do you find a system resembling ours...." The Palestinian people, whether in pre-1967 Israel, East Jerusalem, the West Bank or the Gaza Strip *live* in an occupied country.

CHAPTER TEN

The Prevalence of Torture

The use of torture in Israeli prisons has been the subject of extensive inquiry. In 1977, the London *Sunday Times* conducted a five-month investigation. Corroboration was obtained for the evidence adduced. The torture documented occurred "through the ten years of Israeli occupation" since 1967. The *Sunday Times* study presented the cases of forty-four Palestinians who were tortured. It documented practices in seven centers: prisons within the four principal cities of Nablus, Ramallah, Hebron and Gaza; the interrogation and detention center in Jerusalem known as the Russian Compound or Moscobiya; and special military centers located in Gaza and Sarafand.[135]

The investigation resulted in concrete conclusions: Israeli interrogators routinely ill-treat and torture Arab prisoners. Prisoners are hooded or blindfolded and are hung by their wrists for long periods. Most are struck in the genitals or in other ways sexually abused. Many are sexually assaulted. Others are administered electric shock.

Prisoners are placed in specially constructed "cupboards" two feet square and five feet high with concrete spikes set in the floor. And maltreatment, including "prolonged beatings," is universal in Israeli prisons and detention centers. Torture is so widespread and systematic, concludes the *Sunday Times*, that it cannot be dismissed as the work of "rogue cops" exceeding orders. It is sanctioned as deliberate policy and all Israeli security and intelligence services are involved:

- Shin Bet, equivalent to the F.B.I. and Secret Service in the United States, reports directly to the office of the Prime Minister
- Military Intelligence reports to the Minister of Defense
- Border Police administer all checkpoints. There are checkpoints throughout the territories occupied since 1967, as there are at the borders
- Latam is part of the Department of Special Missions
- A para-military squad is assigned to police units.

Patterns of Torture in Post-'67 Occupied Territories

Each detention center features interrogators with "apparent predilections." The Russian Compound [Moscobiya] interrogators in Jerusalem "favor assaults on the genitals, besides endurance tests such as holding a chair with outstretched arms or standing on one leg."

The specialty of the military center at Sarafand is to blindfold prisoners for long periods, assault them with dogs and hang them by their wrists. The specialty at Ramallah is "anal assault." Electric shock torture is used almost universally.[136]

Fazi Abdel Wahed Nijim was arrested in July 1970. He was tortured at Sarafand and set upon by dogs. Arrested again in July 1973, he was beaten in Gaza prison. Zudhir al-Dibi was arrested in February 1970 and interrogated in Nablus where he was whipped and beaten on the soles of his feet. His testicles were squeezed and he was hosed with ice water.

Shehadeh Shalaldeh was arrested in August 1969 and interrogated at Moscobiya. A ballpoint refill was pushed into his penis. Abed al-Shalloudi was held without trial for sixteen months. Blindfolded and handcuffed while at Moscobiya, he was beaten by Naim Shabo, an Iraqi Jew, Director of the Minorities Department.

Jamil Abu Ghabiyr was arrested in February 1976 and held in Moscobiya. He was beaten on the head, body and genitals and made to lie in ice water. Issam Atif al Hamoury was arrested in October 1976. In Hebron prison the authorities arranged his rape by a prisoner trustee.[137]

In February 1969, Rasmiya Odeh was arrested and brought to Moscobiya. Her father, Joseph, and two sisters were detained for interrogation. Joseph Odeh was kept in one room while Rasmiya was beaten nearby. When they brought him to her she was lying on the floor in blood-stained clothes. Her face was blue, her eye black. In his presence, they held her down and shoved a stick into her vagina. One of the interrogators ordered Joseph Odeh "to fuck" his daughter. When he refused they began beating both him and Rasmiya. They again spread her legs and shoved the stick into her. She was bleeding from the mouth, face and vagina when Joseph Odeh fell unconscious.[138]

The patterns of torture reported by the *Sunday Times* are similar to those found in hundreds of testimonies published by Israeli lawyers, Felicia Langer and Lea Tsemel, by Palestinian lawyers Walid Fahoum and Raja Shehadeh, by Amnesty International and the National Lawyers Guild and the series of accounts this author documented from former prisoners.[139]

This record is established in the West Bank as early as 1968, one year after the occupation began. Although the International Committee of the Red Cross does not, as a rule, make public declarations, it had prepared in 1968 a finding of torture. Its "Report on Nablus Prison" concluded:

"A number of detainees have undergone torture during interrogation by the military police. According to the evidence, the torture took the following forms:
1. Suspension of the detainee by the hands and the simultaneous traction of his other members for hours at a time until he loses consciousness
2. Burns with cigarette stubs
3. Blows by rods on the genitals
4. Tying up and blindfolding for days
5. Bites by dogs
6. Electric shocks at the temples, the mouth, the chest and testicles."[140]

The Case of Ghassan Harb

Ghassan Harb, a 37-year-old Palestinian intellectual and journalist for *Al Fajr,* a prominent Arabic daily, was arrested in 1973. He was taken by Israeli soldiers and two plain-clothes agents from his home to Ramallah prison where he was held fifty days. During this time he was neither interrogated nor accused. He was denied any contact with his family or a lawyer.[141]

On the fiftieth day, Ghassan Harb was taken with a sack over his head to an undisclosed place. Here he was subjected to sustained beating: "Fifteen minutes, twenty minutes beating with his hand across my face."

Stripped naked and a bag placed over his head, he was forced into a confined space. He began to suffocate. He managed by moving his head against the "wall" to remove the bag and found himself in a cupboard-like compartment some 2 feet square and 5 feet high [60 cm. and 150 cm. respectively].

He could neither sit down nor stand up. The floor was concrete with a set of stone spikes set at irregular intervals. They were "sharp with acute edges," 1.5 centimeters high. Ghassan Harb could not stand on them without pain. He had to stand on one leg and then replace it continuously with the other. He was kept in the box for four hours during the first session.

He was then made to crawl on his knees on sharp stones while being beaten for an hour by four soldiers. After being interrogated, Ghassan Harb was returned to his cell and the routine was repeated: beatings, stripping, forced to crawl into a dog kennel two feet square and then the "cupboard." While in the cupboard at night he heard prisoners pleading, "Oh my stomach. You are killing me."

Ghassan Harb's ordeal has been corroborated independently by four people. Mohammed Abu-Ghabiyr, a shoemaker from Jerusalem, described the identical courtyard with its sharp stones and dog kennel. Jamal Freitah, a laborer from Nablus, described the "cupboard" as a "refrigerator" with the same dimensions. It had "a concrete floor with small hills ... with very sharp edges, every one like a nail."

Kaldoun Abdul Haq, a construction company owner from Nablus, also described the courtyard and the "cupboard" with its floor "covered with very sharp stones set in cement." Abdul Haq was hung by his arms from a hook in a wall on the edge of the courtyard.

Husni Haddad, a factory owner from Bethlehem, was made to crawl in the courtyard, the sharp gravel underfoot, and was kicked as he crawled. His box too had "a floor which had spikes like people's thumbs but with sharp edges."

Ghassan Harb was released two-and-a-half years later, never having been charged with a crime or brought to trial. His lawyer, Felicia Langer, succeeded in taking the matter of his maltreatment to the Israeli Supreme Court. No full statements were taken or admitted into the court hearing; no witnesses were called. The court dismissed out of hand all charges of torture.

The Case of Nader Afouri

Nader Afouri was a strong, vital man, the weight-lifting champion of Jordan. When he was released in 1980 after his fifth imprisonment, he could neither see, hear, speak, walk nor control his bodily functions. Between 1967 and 1980, Nader Afouri was held ten and a half years as an administrative detainee. Despite the brutal treatment and torture inflicted upon Nader during five imprisonments, the Israeli authorities could neither extract a confession nor produce any evidence with which to bring Nader Afouri to trial.[142]

The First Imprisonment—1967-1971:

"I was arrested initially in 1967, the first year of the occupation. They took me from my home in Nablus, blindfolded me and hanged me from a helicopter. All the people of Beit Furik and Salem villages near Nablus witnessed this.

"They brought me to Sarafand, the most harsh prison, a military prison. I was the first man from the West Bank or Gaza to be brought there. When they set the helicopter down, they pushed me out and ordered me to run. I heard gunfire and ran as they were shooting at me.

"They took me to a large room full of red, yellow and green lights. I could hear screams and the sounds of beatings. I heard a man yell: 'You'll have to confess.' Then I heard a man confessing. Soon, I discovered this was a recording meant to intimidate me.

"Then they took me to the interrogator. They tied me with chains to green doors. Each door had a pulley. They opened the doors, spreading my hands and legs, then wound the pulleys 'till I fell unconscious.

"They made me get up on a chair, tied my hands to chains hanging from a window and slowly removed the chair. My muscles tore as the weight of my body pulled on my hands. The pain was terrible.

"There were five or six men. They all beat me. They hit me with blows on the head. They chained me to a chair. One would beat me and some of the other men in the room would say 'Stop.' Then they would change from one to the other, each hitting me in turn. I was kept chained in that chair and never allowed to stand up.

"They kept torturing me. An interrogator sucked on a cigarette. When it was red, he placed it on my face, chest and genitals—all over.

"One shoved a pen refill up my penis while the others watched. As they did this they asked me to confess. I started to bleed from my penis and was taken to Ramle Prison Hospital but was soon brought back again to Sarafand for further interrogation.

"I was in Sarafand twelve-and-a-half months and was interrogated continuously. No one can endure twelve-and-a-half months. On four occasions my friends in the other prisons were informed officially that I had died.

"The first month in Sarafand, I was *always* blindfolded and had chains on my hands and legs. After one month they removed the hand chains and blindfold. But I wore leg chains for twelve-and-a-half months. Day and night I had chains on my legs. The marks are still on my ankles.

"This was the routine: They would beat me, interrogate me, then throw me in the cell. I would rest awhile; then they would take me again.

"The cell was 3 feet by 4 feet by 4 feet high [1 meter by 1.3 meters by 1.3 meters]. My height is 5 feet 6 inches [1.7 meters]. I slept crouched with my legs up against my stomach. There were no windows in the cell and no furnishings, only a pot for shitting. I had two blankets. The stones on the floor were very sharp. They punctured my feet when I walked.

"They began to bring other prisoners. They gave us army clothes with numbers on the back. I was number one. They would only call me by my number, never by my name. They were always insulting me, yelling 'Maniuk (Faggot), I will fuck you.' When we were chained outside they brought savage dogs. The dogs jumped at us, grabbed our clothing and bit us.

"Over thirty people were arrested after my own detention and all underwent the same torture. All, however, broke down under torture and wrote confessions and are in prison for life. I didn't confess. The torture destroyed my penis and I could only urinate drop by drop. I could not walk for three-and-a-half months when I finished the interrogation. But I did not confess. I never spoke a word in twelve-and-a-half months."

Nader Afouri was sent to Nablus Prison where he began a hunger strike demanding his freedom. He took only water and a little salt. After ten days he was promised his release. Ten days later when Nader Afouri had not been released, he renewed the hunger strike for yet another week. Again the Administrative Vice-President of Nablus Prison promised to release him. When there was still no action after twenty-five days, Nader Afouri announced another hunger strike.

"I was sent to the cells of Ramle prison after twenty-two days of this hunger strike. Dr. Silvan, the director there, brought several soldiers with him. They beat me on the head. I passed between life and death. They chained my hands and forced a tube in my nose. It was like an electrical shock. I began to shake. I became hysterical when the food reached my throat and began to scream constantly. They gave me an injection in the hip and I relaxed.

"When this torture failed to make me talk I was placed in the Prison Hospital at Ramle and then sent back to Nablus Prison."

Each time a confession was extracted from another prisoner incriminating him, Nader Afouri would be called for interrogation. Often he did not even know the people who spoke against him. But still he did not confess, nor was he brought to trial.

Nader Afouri was well respected in Nablus and became a leader of the prisoners. When Abu Ard, an informer, accused him of leading the other prisoners, Nader Afouri was sent to Tulkarm prison.

On his arrival at Tulkarm, he was beaten on the face by Major Sofer and thrown into a cell with thirty-five other prisoners. Nader Afouri had had enough. When Major Sofer later approached Nader to hit him again, Nader Afouri punched Sofer through the bars of the cell door. When the Prison Director later struck him, Nader Afouri grabbed an ashtray and hit the Director on the head. The army was called. Nader Afouri described the consequences:

"Fifteen soldiers came in and beat me on the head with a chair. I fell unconscious. They put my shirt in my mouth and beat me more. I became hysterical as I was gagging. They gave me an injection and I fell unconscious. I awoke alone in the corridor. I couldn't see.

"All Tulkarm Prison went on strike and the prisoners met with the Director to speak about me. He promised he would release me the next day if they stopped their strike. The Director came the next day and shook hands with me and said: 'I swear by my life that you are a man.' They brought me socks and a jacket and promised me a private visit with my family."

Nader Afouri was not freed. Instead he was sent to Bet Il prison from which he was eventually released in 1971. His four years of imprisonment were without trial and labelled administrative detention.

Only a few months lapsed before Nader Afouri was detained again. His second imprisonment lasted from 1971 until 1972 and a third from November 1972 until 1973.

The Fourth Imprisonment: Nov. 1973 — Nov. 1976:

"Hebron, Moscobiya, Ramallah and Nablus: I stayed three months in a cell in each of these four prisons and the interrogation and torture continued.

"It was snowing during the interrogation in Hebron. They stripped me and put me outside in the cold. They tied me with chains to a pole and poured ice water over me. They let me down and brought me to a fire to warm up only to bring me outside again for the ice water treatment.

"Iron balls were put into my scrotum and squeezed against the testicles. Pain just enveloped me.

"One of the investigators, Abu Haroun, said he would turn my face into a bulldog's. He was scientific. He hit me with rapid punches for two hours. Then he brought a mirror and said: 'Look at your face.' I did indeed look like a bulldog.

"In Nablus they burned me with cigarettes and again pressed the metal balls against my testicles—squeezing the egg against the iron. They used pliers to pull out four of my teeth.

"I was detained three years administratively. During that time as an act of revenge, they also dynamited my house."

The Fifth Imprisonment: November 1978 — 1980:

"They arrested me again in November 1978 and sent me directly to Hebron. They greeted me, sneeringly, declaring: 'We will make you confess from your asshole.' I told them I speak from my mouth, not my asshole.

"At first they spoke nicely to me because they knew torture wouldn't work. Then they brought the men in charge of interrogation: Uri, Abu Haroun, Joni, the Psychiatrist, Abu Nimer who has a finger missing, Abu Ali Mikha and Dr. Jims.

"They chained me to a pole and concentrated their beatings on my chest. They lay me down on the floor and jumped high in the air landing on my chest. Uri did this seven or eight times. It was savage, unending torture for seven days. They smashed their boot heels on my fingernails, breaking my fingers.

"It was snowing so they poured ice water on me. They handed me a paper and gave me two hours to confess. I said I knew nothing. They chained me to a chair. All of them began to beat me with their hands and feet. I fell down. My head was on the floor. I saw Uri fly through the air and I felt his karate chop on my head. This was the last memory I had for two years.

"I have been told that I was dragged back to the cell. The other prisoners had to feed me, clean me and turn me over. I was incontinent and shat on myself. I could not move my hands or walk. I could not hear. I could not recognize anyone. Only my lips could move and I would swallow whatever was put in my mouth. People had to move my head. They had to move my limbs from under my body. My weight fell to 103 pounds [47 kilos].

"Two years later, I woke up in a mental hospital. I had five fractures in my hips and I couldn't walk."

His friends were able to arouse public concern throughout Israel and the Occupied Territories. Israeli officials and journalists wrote that Nader Afouri was "feigning" and that he was an excellent "actor."

But the prisoners who had taken care of him and the journalists and sympathizers who visited him when he was finally transferred from prison to a hospital, as well as the hospital staff that eventually treated him, bore witness to his condition. Nader Afouri became a *cause celebre* for the Palestinian people, a symbol of the torment inflicted upon them and of the heroic dimension of their resistance.

The Case of Dr. Azmi Shuaiby

Azmi Shuaiby, a dentist, was an active member of the El Bireh City Council in the West Bank and an elected representative to the National Guidance Committee. Since 1973, Dr. Shuaiby has been arrested, brutally tortured and imprisoned seven times. Between 1980 and 1986 he was forbidden to leave the limits of El Bireh and was confined to his house after 6 p.m. In 1986, he was again imprisoned and then deported from the West Bank.[143]

He has never been accused of armed actions or of promoting violence. But Dr. Shuaiby refuses Israeli demands that he collaborate. He has written articles against the occupation and settlements and in favor of an independent Palestinian state.

In 1973, when first arrested at the age of twenty, Azmi was told: "We have been watching you. You were first in your class at the University. We can make you a very rich and powerful man in the West Bank. You must cooperate with us and join the Village Leagues." Upon his refusal, the series of arrests and savage torture began. Dr. Shuaiby described the methods of torture, both physical and psychological to which he was subjected.

"They used heavy batons. They put my legs between chair legs so I couldn't move. Then they beat the soles of my feet. My feet swelled. After one minute I could no longer feel my legs. The pain was excruciating. I was unable to stand.

"They would stand behind me. I couldn't tell if anyone were there. Suddenly, the interrogator clapped his hands over my ears with great force. It caused sudden, terrible pressure in my nose, mouth, and ears—a loud ringing which went on for five minutes. I lost my balance and hearing.

"They used a giant guard to punch me constantly. He said: 'You are a dentist? Which hand do you use? If we break your hand you will no longer be a dentist.' Then he beat my hand until I felt it break.

"They tied my hands behind my back and suspended me on a hook.

They spread my legs and beat me on the testicles with sticks. Then they squeezed my testicles. I cannot describe the agony produced by squeezing the testicles. You feel stabbing pain in your stomach, in all your nerves. You want to faint.

"They put me outside in the winter, naked and fully exposed, with my cuffed hands suspended from hooks. I was hung this way from 11 p.m. at night until just before sunrise. Then I was returned to my cell. They had put water on the cell floor so that I couldn't sleep.

"They told me I must collaborate with them and that when I did I must tell neither the Red Cross nor anyone else that I was working for them. I replied: 'OK, I will tell them that you said I must not tell anyone you want me to work for you.' I refused to collaborate. They beat me endlessly."

In 1980, the Israelis introduced new techniques. Dr. Shuaiby designates these methods "psychological torture;" he found them harder to endure than the physical torment. "Your brain is affected."

Dr. Azmi Shuaiby was subjected to the following ordeal:

Isolation: "No one was allowed to speak to me, not even the soldiers. The cell was 4.5 feet by 5.5 feet and 9 feet high [1.5m by 1.8m by 3m]. In one corner was a stinking hole used as a toilet. There was only a tiny window near the floor. I could never see the sky. The bare light was on day and night. I had nothing to read. I heard no voices. Food was put in the corner and the door opened very slightly. I had to strain to reach for it piece by piece.

"The bedding consisted of a plastic cover less than one half inch [1 cm.] thick. It was always wet. Once a week I was allowed to go out for a few minutes to air the bedding. No soldier was permitted to speak to me.

"To maintain my sanity I collected small pieces of orange peel and made shapes with them. I would ask myself questions and then answer them. I also pulled threads from the blanket and knit them together."

The Cupboard: "I was entombed for four days and nights, squeezed into a bent but standing position in a cupboard 20 inches by 20 inches [50cm. by 50cm.]. It was very dark. A filthy sack had been tied over my head. My hands were handcuffed behind my back with special cuffs. If I moved my hands in any way the cuffs automatically tightened. I was unable to move in the cupboard. I had to sleep while standing. I slept a minute at a time, awakening abruptly, convinced that I was suffocating."

The Interrogators: "The interrogation and torture were carried out by a team. All were officers and captains, their names Gadi, Edi, Sami, Yacob and Dany. The interrogation room is their kingdom; no one can enter.

"During the 1982 Israeli invasion of Lebanon, the interrogation team was sent to Lebanon and a new staff brought to the West Bank prisons. The "new" staff consisted of former torturers. One man had been an interrogator ten years before; now he was a businessman.

"Captain Dany returned from Lebanon during my imprisonment. Captain Dany is a very tall, handsome man of thirty-five years. He is very crude, constantly yelling 'Fuck your sister, fuck your mother.' He would force my mouth open and spit in it. In 1973, he tried to force a bottle into my anus. When he saw me on his return from Lebanon, he said: 'Oh, Azmi is here,' and proceeded to tell me about the young children in Ansar. 'I interrogate children 10, 11 and 12,' he began, giving me accounts of their beatings.

Dr. Azmi Shuaiby was imprisoned three times in 1982. Between December 7, 1981, and January 16, 1982, he was kept in isolation during the General Strike in the West Bank and the closure of Bir Zeit University. From April 1 to May 3, when the Israelis disbanded the West Bank City Councils, Azmi was placed in the "cupboard" and then again in isolation. He was kept in isolation throughout the Israeli invasion of Lebanon.

"Recently they told me: 'We will destroy your clinic by jailing you every alternate month. Our computer will determine when you are scheduled to be imprisoned again.'"

In 1986, Dr. Azmi Shuaiby was deported.

The Case of Mohammed Manasrah

Mohammed Manasrah was a trade union activist, secretary of the Bethlehem University Student Senate and is currently a writer and journalist. He was imprisoned three times for a total of four-and-a-half years and then placed on additional probation for two years. His torture during interrogation was unrelenting, resulting in sexual dysfunction and hearing loss. He also endured numerous additional briefer detentions as well as house arrest and town restrictions.[144]

The First Imprisonment:

"I was nineteen years old in 1969 when I was arrested for the first time. I was taken with a group of people and held in the Moscobyia [the Russian Compound in Jerusalem] for six months, where I was interrogated about demonstrations, publications and organizations.

"Moscobiya was barbaric. They took our clothes and covered our eyes. They cuffed our hands and chained ten of us in a row. We were stripped naked. They threw water on us. Then they beat us in turn, using sticks on our heads and on our sexual organs. They would alternate throwing water on us and beating us on our sexual organs. We would hear them filling the buckets and brace ourselves, but no matter how we tried, we could never prepare ourselves for the beatings.

"My friend, Bashir al Kharya, a lawyer, has been in prison since 1969. They beat his head with heavy sticks for three days. His head became green from mold and was infected with bacteria for five years. He is still held in Tulkarm Prison.

The Second Imprisonment:

"In 1971, the authorities accused me of membership in both the P.F.L.P. (Popular Front for the Liberation of Palestine) and Fatah [Yasir Arafat's group in the P.L.O.] even though one couldn't be a member of both organizations.

"The security services lacked any evidence but they gave me the choice of being charged with membership in an illegal organization and being sentenced to prison or voluntarily moving to Amman [Jordan]. I told them I would rather be imprisoned for a lifetime than be exiled. I confessed to membership in the United Student Council, the council of all student organizations which had been declared illegal. I was then imprisoned for one year in Ramallah and Nablus prisons.

The Third Imprisonment:

"In 1975, they raided my house in Dheisheh camp and confiscated all my books. They brought me to Bassa Police Station where they beat me for two days. They asked no questions. One interrogator stood in front of me and another behind me. Suddenly the one behind would clap his hands with great force on both my ears. Blood flowed from my ears and mouth. I suffered brain damage. One prisoner, whom they were trying to terrify, fainted when they brought him to where I was being tortured.

"They imprisoned me for three years. I was held in Hebron, Ramallah, again in Hebron, Farguna, Beersheba, again in Hebron and then again in Beersheba. They would transfer me for 'security reasons' as punishment after hunger strikes."

Torture in Hebron Prison:

Mohammed Manasrah was taken to Hebron and tortured in many

different ways:

"They tied me upside down and beat me endlessly on the feet with a piece of wood. You can't imagine how much they hit me. My feet swelled to a huge size and turned blue. I bled under the skin.

"They stripped me of my clothes and hung me by chains with my hands above my head and my feet barely touching the ground. They beat me constantly on the feet, always concentrating on my feet. Sometimes they would let me down and put my feet into a basin of filthy, stinking cold water. This would relieve the pain. Then they would hang me up again. I had to sleep chained up, with my hands above my head. This went on for fourteen days.

"Maisara Abul Hamdia was with me. For every blow I received, he got two. Maisara would be hanging when I entered the torture room. Then Maisara would find me hanging when he was brought to the torture room. [Maisara was later deported to Jordan.]

"After fourteen days, I would lose consciousness constantly. I was put in Cell #5. It was 5 feet 3 inches by 2 feet and 5 feet 6 inches high [160cm. by 60cm. by 168cm.]. It was as high as I am tall and its length was such that I had to put my legs on the wall when I lay down.

"The only sound I ever heard was that of the keys. I became terrified whenever I heard that sound. I don't know exactly how long I was there. It was somewhere between five days and one week.

"I was beaten all night when they transferred me from Cell #5 to Cell #4. They used wide sticks and beat me on the head and sexual organs. They pulled my hair and hit my head on the wall. I have a permanent problem with my sexual organs and have had many X-Rays taken of my head and sexual organs.

"I was brought to the military courtroom early in the morning and made to wait all day. But there was no session. Instead, Abu Ghazal, the famous interrogator, came. He grabbed my hair and swung me around the room, smashing me against the wall. My hair was pulled out. He threatened to send me to Sarafand or "Akka" [a secret prison used in 1974 and 1975] if I didn't confess within two days.

"I was put in a cell and slept the entire time. I didn't know if it were day or night, two days or ten. I still feel cold when I recall this period. I get chills in my legs.

"After two days, ten soldiers rushed into my cell and started to beat me. They dragged me along the floor to the torture room. They told me that my friends and comrades had confessed. I said: 'Bring them to me.' I knew these were lies. They brought two types of people to me in order to make me confess: kind, weak people who couldn't bear to see how I was being tortured and 'asafir' [spies].

"Now they initiated other methods—alternating between beatings and soft talk in the hope that I would crack and 'confess.' They accused me of being a member of the P.F.L.P., Fatah and the Communist Party. They would change their accusation, but one thing remained constant: after each accusation—they would beat me savagely.

"They brought two Majors to see me who lectured me for six hours about the Soviet Union's crimes against the Jews and China's oppression of its national minorities. They accused me of being a communist because they found books on Marxism in my house. I told them there couldn't be peace here without self-determination for the Palestinian people. They asked me to write this down and sign it and I did.

"After forty-six days of interrogation and detention they sent me to a military court in Ramallah. I was accused of having carried out actions against the authorities. My lawyer, Ghozi Kfir, asked for specifics. The court responded: 'This is a revolutionary and a deceiver.'

"Before the hearing my lawyer and the prosecutor had worked out a deal. I was to be released without charge if I *did not* speak in court about how I was tortured. But the judge ignored the agreement and sentenced me to five years. I served three years and was placed on probation for two."

House Arrest and Municipal Restriction:

The Shin Bet harassed Mohammed Manasrah after he was released from prison. They approached every employer for whom he worked and told them to fire him. Mohammed Manasrah lost four jobs before becoming a full-time trade union organizer.

On January 7, 1982, Mohammed Manasrah was ordered to return from Bethlehem to Wadi Fukin, the small village of his birth located inside the pre-1967 border. He was placed under house arrest in Wadi Fukin for six months. He had no income and had to depend upon his neighbors' help.

The authorities and the Village League [collaborators] threatened Mohammed Manasrah, his family and all with whom he came in contact. His house was raided many times; books and papers were taken. His family was prevented from travelling to the West Bank. His brother's work permit was removed. His sister-in-law was attacked by the Village League when they mistook her for Mohammed's wife.

The Military Governor threatened every family whose sons visited him. The young men were investigated. Three teachers from the elementary school were interrogated after such visits. "They installed a siege around me: economic, social and psychic."

Mohammed Manasrah, in defiance of the municipal restriction, returned to Bethlehem where at least his wife was able to work. "My brother and his child were arrested in order to pressure me to return to Wadi Fukin, but I remained in Bethlehem."

His house arrest was eventually transferred to Bethlehem. "I couldn't stay home long. I went here and there. The soldiers grabbed me and took me to prison."

On December 1, 1982, a new military order permitted him to move within the municipal borders, but he was not allowed to work. He was obliged to report to the Military Governor each day and remain there until noon.

After a year, the restrictions ended. Less than one month later, the Military Governor ordered a further six-month municipal restriction.

Imprisonment Again:

Mohammed Manasrah entered Bethlehem University in 1983 to study sociology. He was soon elected Secretary of the Student Senate. In November 1983, he and other members of the student organization were imprisoned after sponsoring a Palestinian cultural exhibit.

Torture of Palestinian Youths

Torture is routinely administered to Palestinian youths, whether they are Israeli citizens or residents of the Occupied Territories. Hussam Safieh and Ziad Sbeh Ziad, from the Galilee, were arrested on a charge of raising the Palestinian flag on the first anniversary of the massacre of Sabra and Shatila. Six months later they were released, having been acquitted when no evidence against them could be produced and a confession could not be extracted. In court, the youths spoke of the torture to which they had been subjected while in detention.

They were sprayed with cold water and left naked in a cold room. They were beaten over their entire bodies, including their genitals. Electric torture was used. Ziad, his hands tied behind his back, was thrown back and forth from one interrogator to the next. He was beaten on the face and neck. He refused to sign a confession.[145]

Mu'awyah Fah'd Qawasmi, son of the assassinated mayor of Hebron, Fah'd Qawasmi, and his cousin, Usameh Fayez Qawasmi, were among the 17,000 Palestinian youths detained by the Israelis during the recent uprising in the West Bank and Gaza.

Israeli interrogators poured water on them, hooked clips attached to electric wires to their feet and then turned on the current. Mu'awyah lost consciousness three times during half an hour of electric shock torture.[146] Lawyers who regularly defend those accused of "security" offenses declare unanimously that the Military Courts in Israel and the post-1967 Occupied Territories "collude in and knowingly conceal the use of torture by Israel's intelligence services."[147]

Should defense counsel challenge the validity of the confession or present evidence of torture, a "little trial" or "Zuta" [Hebrew] occurs. The prosecution produces the army or police officer who took down the confession. But, as the Israeli lawyer, Lea Tsemel, observes: "The officer takes the statement, indeed often composes it for the prisoner. But this officer does not conduct the interrogation or perform the torture. Hence he can state that the confession was freely accepted."[148]

Interrogators and warders can rarely be identified and brought to court because they use assumed Arab names such as Abu Sami and Abu Jamil or nicknames such as Jacky, Dany, Edi, Orli, etc. Even when a prisoner succeeds in bringing his torturer to court, there is no result. Lea Tsemel described how, after enormous effort, in which countless obstacles were overcome, the interrogator who had tortured her client was brought into the courtroom. "He just looked at the defendant and said he had never seen him before in his life. That ended the matter."[149]

Wasfi O. Masri succeeded in having five confessions ruled inadmissible—for which he is much admired among lawyers in Israel and the post-1967 Occupied Territories. This, however, does not assure acquittal. The five were from "a total of thousands."

House Arrests and Town Restrictions

Under Regulation 109 of the Defense Emergency Regulations, a Military Governor may force any person to live in any place he designates. He may confine people to their homes or towns. Travel and association may also be restricted. Such penalties are issued for six months, but they can be renewed repeatedly. In some cases, people have been restricted "until further notice."

Those placed under house arrest, town or travel restrictions are neither formally charged nor brought before a court of law. The Military Governor issuing the order is under no obligation to specify the nature of the offense. Although the restricted person has the right to bring his or her case before both a Military Appeals Committee and the Israeli Supreme Court, it is rare for the Court to challenge any decision based upon grounds of "security" and difficult for the victims and their attorneys to prepare a case. The Military Governor will not specify the details of the charge or the evidence supporting it.

Regulation 109 has been used against Palestinians in Israel as well as the territory occupied since 1967. It has been used against intellectuals, journalists, teachers, artists, lawyers, trade unionists, students and political figures, many, but by no means all of whom were outspoken in their criticism of Israeli policies and in their support of self-determination for the Palestinian people. Between January 1980 and May 1982, Amnesty International noted that 136 restriction orders were issued, affecting 77 people;[150] 100 restriction orders were issued in September 1983 after events commemorating the first anniversary of the massacre of Sabra and Shatila;[151] and the policy has continued to date.

CHAPTER ELEVEN

The Prisons

Israeli prisons are essentially political prisons. They contain mainly Palestinians suspected, accused and occasionally—on the basis of coerced confessions—"convicted" of carrying out, abetting or planning acts of resistance, whether peaceful or armed. While statistics for the total prison population are not available, the number of prisoners in maximum-security prisons who are serving long-term sentences consistently hovers around 3,000; thirty Palestinian women are imprisoned in Neve Tertza, not including those women brought from Lebanon. Lawyers estimate that prior to the recent uprising 20,000 Palestinians were imprisoned each year.

Within the pre-1967 borders there are ten prisons, including Kfar Yonah, Ramle Central Prison, Shattah, Damun, Mahaneh Ma'siyahu, Beersheba, Tel Mond (for juveniles), Nafha, Ashkelon and Neve Tertza.

Nine prisons are located in the post-1967 Occupied Territories: Gaza, Nablus, Ramallah, Bethlehem, Fara'a, Jericho, Tulkarm, Hebron and Jerusalem.

There are regional detention centers at Yagur (Jalameh) and Atlit near Haifa, Abu Kabir in Tel Aviv and the Moscobiya (Russian Compound) in Jerusalem. In addition, police headquarters in Haifa, Acre, Jerusalem, Tel Aviv, the eighteen police stations throughout the state and the forty police outposts in the occupied territories are used to detain suspects for interrogation and torture.[152]

Military installations throughout the country also serve as interrogation and torture centers. Prisoners agree that the most savage of these is Armon ha-Avadon known as the "Palace of Hell" and "Palace of the End." It is located at Mahaneh Tzerffin near Sarafand.

Finally, detention camps with only tents for shelter were erected to maintain the large numbers of Palestinian prisoners brought from Lebanon during the 1982 invasion as well as the youths rounded up during the current resistance. Meggido, Ansar II (in Gaza) and Dhariyah have become detention centers notorious for their inhumane conditions and daily routine of torture.

Distinctions in Treatment

The differences between prisons for Palestinians within the post-1967 Occupied Territories and those within pre-1967 Israel, i.e., within the "Green Line," are not great. Ashkelon prison, Nafha prison, the main wing of Beersheba prison and the special wing of Ramle prison, while located within pre-1967 Israel, are major detention centers for Palestinians from the post-1967 Occupied Territories of the West Bank and Gaza. Damun and Tel Mond are used for Palestinian youth.

The physical location of prisons has little bearing on conditions. Israeli prison authorities maintain rigorous segregation between persons held on criminal charges and those convicted of "security offenses," who are political prisoners.

As only a small number of Jews qualify as political prisoners and only a small number of Palestinians, particularly from the Occupied Territories, are criminal offenders, this separation entails de-facto segregation between Jewish prisoners and Palestinian detainees. Neither contact nor communication is allowed. They are either in separate prisons or different wings of the same institution.

Distinctions are also made between Palestinian prisoners from the territory occupied after 1967 and "Israeli Arab" inmates, who are Palestinian and Druze residing in pre-1967 Israel and holding Israeli citizenship. Conditions of imprisonment for prisoners from the West Bank and Gaza are many times worse than those of pre-1967 "Israeli" inmates.

Some, but not all, prisoners from pre-1967 Israel are allowed a bed or mattress. Approximately 70% of these Israeli prisoners enjoy this "privilege." They also may receive one visit every two weeks and send two letters a month. They are allowed three blankets in summer and five in winter.

Prisoners from the post-1967 Occupied Territories sleep on the floor during summer *and* winter. They are allowed a rubber mat one-quarter of an inch [0.5 cm.] thick, one visit and one post card a month.

Whereas the average living space per prisoner in European and American prisons is 112.5 square feet [$10.5m^2$], in prisons for Palestinians from the West Bank and Gaza, it is one tenth this area or 16 square feet [$1.5m^2$] per prisoner.

The prison bureaucracy is a law unto itself. Upon entering this domain the citizen loses all rights. He or she becomes subject to wholly arbitrary authority wielded by people selected for their harshness.

The Prison Ordinance (revised 1971) has 114 clauses. There is no clause or sub-clause defining prisoner rights. The ordinance provides a legally binding set of rules for the Minister of the Interior, but the Minister himself formulates these rules by administrative decree. There is no provision stipulating obligations incumbent upon the authorities nor is there any clause guaranteeing prisoners a minimum standard of life.

In Israel, it is legally permissible to intern twenty inmates in a cell no more than 15 feet [5m.] long, 12 feet [4m.] wide and 9 feet [3m.] high. This space includes an open lavatory. Prisoners may be confined indefinitely to such cells for twenty-three hours a day.

The Kutler Report

An extensive inquiry into the physical conditions inside prisons located within pre-1967 Israel was published in *Ha'aretz* in 1978 by Israeli journalist, Yair Kutler. Yair Kutler called prison life in Israel "hell on earth" and proceeded to describe each prison in detail.[153] His account is harrowing:

Kfar Yonah: Senior officials name the prison of Kfar Yonah as "Kevar Yonah" (the grave of Yonah). It is the detention center that terrifies all who pass through its gates. Detainees have named it "Meurat Petanim" or "The Lair of Cobras."

"The reception awaiting those remanded there until trial is frightening." Cells are extremely cold and damp. The shabby, torn and filthy mattresses are crowded. Most detainees have nowhere to lie but the floor. The overwhelming stench of human excretion, sweat and filth never fades from the locked and bolted cells. In 'D' wing there are three rooms into which twelve, eighteen and twenty detainees are crammed.

Central Prison of Ramle: Ramle is one of the harshest prisons in Israel. It is a former British police station that was once used as a stable for horses. It is overcrowded and stinking, packed with seven hundred inmates. Many prisoners do not have a bed, a small corner or even a few square meters for themselves. Frequently one hundred men must lie on the floor.

There are twenty-one isolation cells ('X's) in Ramle. Sunlight never penetrates into the isolation cells, which are completely sealed off. A dangling bulb gives off light the whole day long.

In addition to the isolation cells, Ramle has a series of dungeons. They are 6 feet long, 3 feet wide and 6 feet high [2m. by 80cm. by

2m.]. They are dark, filthy and give off a terrible stench. There are no windows or light bulbs; a small opening in the door lets in a little of the light from the corridor.

Before a prisoner is placed in the dungeon cell he is stripped naked and given a torn, thin overall. Once a day he may be let out to use the toilet; otherwise he must contain himself for the entire day and night. He can urinate through a wire mesh in the door. The prisoner is allowed neither a daily walk nor a shower.

Frequently there are beatings. The favored mode is the "blanket method." A few guards cover the prisoner's head and beat him until he falls unconscious.

In order to avoid solitary confinement a prisoner must know how to lead a life of total submission and self-abasement.

Damun: Life in Damun is "hell on earth." "The living conditions are disgraceful and cause revulsion in every visitor who comes to this God forsaken place." The buildings absorb the damp and cold. Five blankets would not be sufficient to keep warm. "Many are sick and most are despairing."

The youth wing of Damun has even worse conditions. Overcrowding is so terrible that youths can only stretch their limbs for two hours every fortnight and this interval is often missed.

Shattah: Overcrowding is terrible in Shattah. The stench is felt at a far distance....The cells are dark, damp and chilly. The air is suffocating. In summer during the period of great heat in the Beit Shean valley, the prison is a blazing hell.

Sarafand: The "Palace of the End" is set behind a high wire fence seen by all tourists as they drive on the last section of road from Jerusalem to Tel Aviv, but five miles from Ben Gurion airport. This is the perimeter of Sarafand which is ten miles square and Israel's largest army ordinance and supply depot. It is also the repository of the Jewish National Fund, which uses Sarafand to store equipment for construction of new settlements in pre-1967 Israel and the post-1967 Occupied Territories.

The inexorable relationship between occupation, settlement, colonization and the system of torture visited upon Palestinians becomes evident. Sarafand—the torture center—has historical significance.

It was built prior to World War II and served as the principal ordinance depot for Britain. It was one of the most notorious camps for detainees during the Palestinian uprising in 1936 against British rule and Zionist colonization of the land. The old British Mandate buildings were simply taken over by Israeli authorities, their function unaltered, and used for a new generation of Palestinian detainees. The center, known by Palestinian and Jew alike during the British era as the "concentration camp," has been maintained in character and use.

Nafha—A Political Prison: Palestinian political prisoners have not received the status of Prisoners of War but prisoner camps are constructed for them. Nafha is called "the political prison" by its inhabitants.

It is in the desert, eight kilometers from Mitzoe Ramon and halfway between Beersheba and Eilat. It is in a barren area with terrible sandstorms. Sand penetrates everything. Nights are extremely cold and the daytime heat is unbearable. Snakes and scorpions roam the cells.

A typical cell is 18 feet by 9 feet [6m. by 3m.]. There are ten mattresses on the floor and no other space. A primitive lavatory occupies one corner. Above the lavatory is a shower. While one prisoner uses the toilet, others must wash themselves or their dishes. In a room such as this, ten prisoners spend twenty-three hours a day. One half hour a day all the prisoners must walk in a small concrete yard 15 feet by 45 feet [5m. by 15m.]

Many prisoners are ill, suffering from the effects of repeated torture and brutal prison living conditions.[154]

Daily Practice in Israeli Prisons

Political prisoners have frequently declared that the conditions in the detention centers and prisons both in pre-1967 Israel and the post-1967 Occupied Territories are designed to destroy them both physically and psychically.

Beatings: In all prisons in pre-1967 Israel and the Occupied Territories prisoners are beaten. In Ramle, this is performed in the dungeons or "isolation cells:" A number of warders attack the prisoner and beat him with their fists, boots and clubs made from wooden hoe handles which are kept in a closet adjacent to the dungeon cells.

In Damun prison, beating is done more primitively. It is performed in public in the courtyard. The most brutal guards are in charge of the "Post." This is the prisoner transport vehicle which makes three trips weekly from the detention center in Abu Kabir to Shattah prison. It stops at all prisons inside Israel except Ashkelon and Beersheba. Every trip of the "Post" results in savage beatings. Given the slightest pretext, Post guards take the victim off the vehicle at the next Post stations and "beat him beyond recognition."

Isolation: Isolation is not regarded as punishment under the law. In reality, few people can survive many months in cells 3 feet [1 m.] by 8 feet [2.5m.] for twenty-three hours a day. Yet no prisoner who has made any verbal attempt to preserve self-respect has avoided periods in the isolation cells.

Labor: Prison labor is forced labor. It is organized as "a means to harass the lives of prisoners."[155] Political prisoners are deliberately assigned production of boots for the Israeli army, camouflage nets, etc.. Those who refuse are denied such "privileges" as cash for the canteen, time out of cells, books or newspapers and writing materials. Some are punished with isolation.

The average wage for this labor is $.05 per hour. Forced labor is deployed to maximize physical and emotional stress. It is also a means of exploitation.

Food: Nutrition in prisons is deficient and food budgets are minimal. Allocated meat, vegetables and fruits are often sequestered by the staff. Eggs, milk and a fresh tomato are categorized as prisoner luxuries.

Medical Treatment: In 1975, a prisoner in Damun prison cut his wrists and legs. Fellow inmates called the guard. A delegation of three guards arrived. The medical orderly opened the cell and grabbed the prisoner and without uttering a word clubbed the man's face repeatedly. The prisoner fell to the floor; the medical worker kicked him incessantly.

Prisoners are jailed in unsuitable buildings. They suffer in summer from exhausting heat. In winter the damp penetrates "to the bone." In Ramle prison during winter, one-third of the prison population suffers from swelling of the hands and feet due to severe chill. The only medication available is vaseline, but even it is rarely allowed.

Detainees who serve sentences of more than a few months leave prison with permanent disabilities. Lighting conditions are so poor that prisoners suffer from deterioration of eyesight. Kidney ailments and ulcers have an incidence among inmates five times that of the general population.

Asafir: Since 1977, prisoners have reported that torture is also administered by a small group of collaborators in each prison, some of whom are not actual prisoners but informers posing as such. Whether prisoners who collaborate or informers insinuated into the prison, the procedure has been institutionalized. In each prison and detention center, special rooms are set aside for the collaborators, who are known as "asafir" or "song birds." Common among the "asafir" are violent criminals selected for their fierceness. Others are selected from those held on political charges, even though they lack a political past. The latter are allowed privileges in accordance with the services they perform.

Not Isolated Cases

While much is made of the democratic and humanist pretensions of Israel, the evidence presented here, as does the evidence accumulated in all studies of Zionist colonization and rule in Palestine, strips away this facade.

The individual cases examined here are not isolated nor are they the result of extraordinary circumstances. The cases cited do not differ fundamentally from others. The torturers are not aberrant individual cops who get out of hand. They are members of *all* sections of Israeli police and security divisions operating in the line of duty.

Violence is the norm for dealing with Palestinians, whether they are farmers taking their produce to market or youths throwing stones, Palestinian citizens of pre-1967 Israel or Palestinian residents of the territories occupied in 1967 and afterward. Torture is a fundamental part of the legal system, coercion is the route to confession and confession is fundamental to conviction.

The treatment of prisoners does not change with the particular party in power. If Prime Minister Menachem Begin categorized Palestinians as "two legged beasts," the systematic brutality imposed upon the Palestinian detainee is just as severe under the Labor Alignment governments. As former Prime Minister David Ben Gurion said, "The Military regime exists to defend the right of Jewish settlement everywhere."[156]

CHAPTER TWELVE

Strategy for Conquest

In 1982, while advance preparations were being completed for the invasion of Lebanon and the massacre of Palestinians in the camps around Beirut, Sidon and Tyre, a remarkable document was published in *Kivunim (Directions)*, the journal of the Department of Information of the World Zionist Organization. Its author, Oded Yinon, was formerly attached to the Foreign Ministry and reflects high-level thinking in the Israeli military and intelligence establishment.

The article, "A Strategy for Israel in the 1980's," outlines a timetable for Israel to become the imperial regional power based upon the dissolution of the Arab states. In discussing the vulnerability of the corrupt regimes of the Middle East, Yinon inadvertently exposes the full measure of their betrayal of the needs of the population and their inability to defend themselves or their people against imperial subjugation.

Divide and Rule

Yinon revives the idea of former Labor Foreign Minister Abba Eban that the Arab East is a "mosaic" of ethnic divergence. The form of rule, therefore, appropriate to the region is the Millet system of the Ottoman Empire, wherein administrative rule was based upon local functionaries presiding over discrete ethnic communities.

"This world with its ethnic minorities, its factions and internal crises, which is astonishingly self-destructive, as we can see in Lebanon, in non-Arab Iran and now also in Syria, is unable to deal successfully with its fundamental problems."[157]

Yinon contends that the Arab nation is a fragile shell waiting to be shattered into multiple fragments. Israel must follow through with the policies it has pursued since the inception of Zionism, seeking to purchase local agents among factions and communal groups who will assert themselves against other such communities at Israel's behest. This will always be feasible, argues Yinon, because:

"The Moslem Arab world is built like a temporary house of cards, put together by foreigners (France and Britain in the 1920's), without the wishes and desires of the inhabitants having been taken into account. It was arbitrarily divided into nineteen states, all made of combinations of minorities and ethnic groups which are hostile to one another, so that every Arab Moslem state nowadays faces ethnic social destruction from within, and in some a civil war is already raging."[158] [Most of the Arabs, 118 million out of 170 million today, live in Africa, primarily in Egypt (45 million).]

The "new" strategy of the eighties is the old imperial dictum of divide and rule, which depends for its success upon the securing of corrupt satraps to do the bidding of an aspiring imperial order.

"In this giant and fractured world there are a few wealthy groups and a huge mass of poor people. Most of the Arabs have an average yearly income of $300. Lebanon is torn apart and its economy is falling to pieces; there is no centralized power, but only five de-facto sovereign authorities."[159]

Dissolving Lebanon

Lebanon was the model, prepared for its role by the Israelis for thirty years, as the Sharett diaries revealed. It is the expansionist compulsion set forth by Herzl and Ben Gurion even as it is the logical extension of the Sharett diaries. The dissolution of Lebanon was proposed in 1919, planned in 1936, launched in 1954 and realized in 1982.

"Lebanon's total dissolution into five provinces serves as a precedent for the entire Arab world including Egypt, Syria, Iraq and the Arabian peninsula and is already following that track. The subsequent dissolution of Syria and Iraq into ethnically or religiously unique areas, as in Lebanon, is Israel's primary target on the Eastern front in the long run. The dissolution of the military power of these states serves as the primary short-term target.[160]

Fragmenting Syria

"Syria will fall apart, in accordance with its ethnic and religious structure, into several states such as in present day Lebanon, so that there will be a Shi'ite Alawi state along its coast, a Sunni state in the Aleppo area, another Sunni state in Damascus hostile to its northern neighbor and the Druze who will set up a state, maybe even in our Golan [the Golan Heights was occupied by Israel in 1967], and certainly in the Hauran and in northern Jordan. This state of affairs will be the guarantee for peace and security in the area in the long run, and that aim is aready within our reach today."161

Each Arab state is examined with a view to assessing how it may be disassembled. Wherever minority religious groupings are present in the army, Yinon sees opportunity. Syria is singled out in this respect.

"The Syrian army today is mostly Sunni with an Alawi officer corps, the Iraqi army Shi'ite with Sunni commanders. This has great significance in the long run, and that is why it will not be possible to retain the loyalty of the army for a long time."162

Yinon proceeds to examine how the "civil war," which had been inflicted on Lebanon by means of financing Major Sa'ad Haddad in the Lebanese South and the Gemayels' Phalange around Beirut, may be extended to Syria.

"Syria is fundamentally no different from Lebanon except in the strong military regime which rules it. But the real civil war taking place nowadays between the Sunni majority and the Shi'ite Alawi ruling minority (a mere 12% of the population) testifies to the severity of the domestic trouble."163

The Assault on Iran

The revolutionary insurgency against the Shah of Iran—one of the principal clients of American imperialism, imposed by a C.I.A. coup in 1953—appeared to open the road to revolution throughout the Middle East. Not only did Israel and its U.S. patron fear the appeal to Shi'ite Muslims throughout the region—who tended to be among the poor and disadvantaged—but the challenge to U.S. domination struck a chord amongst the masses in each ethnic group and nation.

This was the background to the unleashing of an attack by Iraq on Iran's southern province, Khuzistan, where the oil production and refineries were located. Like Yinon, Israeli and U.S. planners calculated that since Iran's oil rich province was populated by Iran's Arab minority, the province could be detached from Iran relatively easily. An attack by Iraq was expected to be met by sympathy from the Arab minority of Khuzistan. Iran is a nation consisting of ethnic groupings: 15 million Persians (Farsi), 12 million Turks, 6 million Arabs, 3 million Kurds, Baluchi, Turkmeni and smaller nationalities.

"Almost half of Iran's population is comprised of a Persian-speaking group and the other half of an ethnically Turkish group. Turkey's population comprises a Turkish Sunni Moslem majority (some

50%) and two large minorities, 12 million Shi'ite Alawis and 6 million Sunni Kurds. In Afghanistan there are 5 million Shi'ites who constitute one-third of the population. In Sunni Pakistan there are 15 million Shi'ites who endanger the existence of that state."[164]

The assumption was that Iran, too, could be fragmented, severing the oil producing provinces through invasion. Khomeini had continued the Shah's policies of oppressing national minorities and the repression visited upon the Arab minority by Khomeini's provincial governor, Admiral Madani, encouraged the C.I.A. and Israeli Mossad to push the Iraqi regime to invade.

As with the other regimes of the Arab East, rhetoric aside, the military oligarchies and monarchies in power are available to the highest bidder. But the oil workers in Abadan and Ahwaz, the refining cities of Iran's Khuzistan province, were highly politicized. They had been the backbone of the National Front when Mossadegh nationalized the Anglo-Iranian Oil Corporation in 1952, and the Communist Party of Iran (Tudeh) had a strong presence among the oil workers. It was the general strike led by the oil workers which was decisive in the Iranian revolution which overthrew the Shah in 1979.

Iraq's invasion backfired. The Arab minority saw it as an attack on the revolution itself. U.S. and Israeli policy now turned to arming both sides, drawing out the war as long as possible, while preventing an Iranian victory.

Yinon is clear about the strategy: "Every kind of inter-Arab confrontation will assist us in the short run and will shorten the way to the more important aim of breaking up Iraq into denominations as in Syria and in Lebanon."[165]

The United States and the Saudi monarchy (which also supports Syria with a $10 billion subsidy) have coordinated an arms blockade of Iran and the massive supply of arms to Iraq. The Egyptian and Jordanian regimes lead the way in support for Iraq. Meanwhile the Soviet Union and the United States each arm Iraq, as the Soviet bureaucratic leadership seeks to use its influence on the Arab regimes to position itself to make sphere of influence arrangements with U.S. rulers—at the expense of the Arab masses who continue to live in poverty.

Targeting Iraq

Yinon makes explicit Israeli motives in arming Khomeini while the United States arms Iraq: "Iraq, rich in oil on the one hand and internally torn on the other, is guaranteed as a candidate for Israel's targets. Its dissolution is even more important for us than that of Syria. Iraq is stronger than Syria. In the short run it is Iraqi power which constitutes the greatest threat to Israel. An Iraqi-Iranian war will tear Iraq apart and cause its downfall at home even before it is able to organize a struggle on a wide front against us."[166]

Advanced preparations are in place as the Zionists plan the fragmentation of Iraq in civil war. "The seeds of inner conflict and civil war are apparent today already, especially after the rise of Khomeini to power in Iran, a leader whom the Shi'ites in Iraq view as their natural leader."[167]

In discussing the weaknesses of Arab society under the present regimes, Yinon, inadvertently, underlines the extent to which the population is left out of the equation of power and decision making, the unrepresentative nature of the Arab regimes, their consequent vulnerability and the futility of their attempts to protect themselves from Zionist expansion by dependence on U.S. power and influence. When all is said and done, they are all being measured for the same fate. What is at issue is not if, but when:

"Iraq is, once again, no different in essence from its neighbors, although its majority is Shi'ite and the ruling minority, Sunni. Sixty-five percent of the population has no say in politics, in which an elite of twenty percent holds the power. In addition, there is a large Kurdish minority in the north, and if it weren't for the strength of the ruling regime, the army and the oil revenues, Iraq's future state would be no different than that of Lebanon in the past or of Syria."[168]

The plan to dissolve the Iraqi state is not algebraic. Israel has marked out the number of statelets, where they are to be located and over whom they are to preside.

"In Iraq, a division into provinces along ethnic/religious lines as in Syria during Ottoman times is possible. So, three (or more) states will exist around the three major cities: Basra, Baghdad and Mosul, and Shi'ite areas in the south will separate from the Sunni and Kurdish north."[169]

Israel seeks to take full advantage of the impact of poverty and the consequent instability of the regimes which must control an alienated population. In this regard the desire of the Zionists to destabilize the Arab regimes and fragment their countries, while not unwelcome to the United States, is met by Pentagon caution as to timing and implementation. There is the constant danger that the wars and manipulated internal divisions required by Zionism and U.S. imperialism to control the region may unleash a popular uprising, as in Iran—and now within the West Bank and Gaza.

The specter of revolutionary change haunts both Israeli and American rulers. It is a prospect, as well, which underlines the critical importance of a revolutionary leadership which will see the struggle through to the end. The P.L.O.'s attempts, for example, to solicit support from the oppressive regimes of the region instead of appealing directly to their suffering populations have led the P.L.O. from one blind alley to another.

The default in leadership is commensurate with the opportunities lost. Describing the oppression meted out by Arab regimes to their own national minorities, Yinon observes: "When this picture is added to the economic one, we see how the entire region is built like a house of cards, unable to withstand its severe problems."[170]

Every country analyzed reveals, essentially, the same set of conditions. "All the Arab states east of Israel are torn apart, broken up and riddled with inner conflict even more than those of the Maghreb (North Africa)."[171]

Double-Crossing Mubarak

The cynicism with which the Zionists discuss the fiction of their concern for "security" is nowhere more transparent than in Yinon's assessment of Egypt. The emergence of Sadat after Israel's seizure of the Sinai, West Bank, Gaza and Golan Heights in 1967 presented the United States with the opportunity to prevent the most populous Arab state from remaining an obstacle to Israeli expansion and American control. The removal of Egypt from opposition was a devastating blow, not merely to the Palestinian people but to the entire Arab population.

The return of Egypt to a degree of dependency on imperialism unknown in the days of Farouk was deeply unpopular among Egyptians. The United States has provided Egypt with nearly $3 billion in aid, loans and disguised subsidy—second only to Israel itself—which underlines the role of the Mubarak government. Yet living standards plummet.

By legitimizing the Israeli colonial state, Sadat betrayed not only the Palestinian people but left the Arab East prey to the designs set forth by Oded Yinon.

What emerges clearly from his strategic analysis is that for the Zionist movement everything is on a timetable, each area marked for conquest or re-conquest and perceived as a target of opportunity, awaiting only the proper relation of forces and the cover of war.

"Egypt, in its present domestic political picture is already a corpse, all the more so if we take into account the growing Moslem-Christian rift. Breaking Egypt down territorially into distinct geographical regions is the political aim of Israel in the Nineteen Eighties on its Western front."[172]

Sadat's return of Egypt to its neo-colonial status under Farouk was rewarded by the recovery of the Sinai. In Israeli eyes, however, not for long.

"Israel will be forced to act directly or indirectly in order to regain control over Sinai as a strategic economic and energy reserve for the long run. Egypt does not constitute a military strategic problem due to its internal conflicts, and it could be driven back to the post-1967 war situation in no more than one day."[173]

Yinon now proceeds to apply the same scalpel to Egypt with which he has already sliced up Lebanon, Syria and Iraq:

"Egypt is divided and torn apart into many foci of authority. If Egypt falls apart, countries like Libya, Sudan or even the more distant states will not continue to exist in their present form and will join the downfall and dissolution of Egypt. The vision of a Christian Coptic state in Upper Egypt alongside a number of weak states with very localized power and without a centralized government is the key to a historical development which was only set back by the peace agreement but which seems inevitable in the long run."[174]

Camp David, then, was a tactical ploy preparatory to the dissolution of Egypt and of the Sudan:

"Sudan, the most torn apart state in the Arab Moslem world today is built upon four groups hostile to each other: an Arab Moslem Sunni minority which rules over a majority of non-Arab Africans, Pagans, and Christians. In Egypt there is a Sunni Moslem majority facing a large minority of Christians which is dominant in upper Egypt: some seven million of them. They will want a state of their own, something like a 'second' Christian Lebanon in Egypt."[175]

It was in Egypt that Gamal Abdel Nasser had overthrown King Farouk and galvanized the Arab world with his vision of Arab unity. But it was a unity based not on revolutionary struggle throughout the region but on an illusory federation between oligarchical regimes.

Tomorrow the Saudis

If Nasser's Egypt finished up, in Israel's vision, "torn apart" like a second Lebanon, Saudi Arabia will be far more vulnerable, for the Monarchy's days are considered numbered.

"The entire Arabian peninsula is a natural candidate for dissolution due to internal and external presures, and the matter is inevitable, especially in Saudi Arabia.

"All the Gulf principalities and Saudi Arabia are built upon a delicate house of sand in which there is only oil. In Kuwait, the Kuwaitis constitute only a quarter of the population. In Bahrain, the Shi'ites are the majority but are deprived of power. In the United Arab Emirates, Shi'ites are once again the majority but the Sunnis are in power."[176]

Nor is there much doubt that as goes Arabia so goes the Gulf:

"The same is true of Oman and North Yemen. Even in the Marxist [sic] South Yemen there is a sizable Shi'ite minority. In Saudi Arabia half the population is foreign, Egyptian and Yeminite, but a Saudi minority holds power."[177]

Depopulating Palestine

Yinon reserves his most relentless assessment for the Palestinians themselves. He is emphatic in acknowledging that the Palestinian people have never relinquished their desire and will to be sovereign in their country; it is all of Palestine over which Zionism must rule.

"Within Israel the distinction between the areas of '67 and the territories beyond them, those of '48, has always been meaningless for Arabs and nowadays no longer has any significance for us."[178]

Not only must Palestinians be driven out of the West Bank and Gaza, but from the Galilee and pre-1967 Israel. They are to be scattered as they were in 1948.

"Dispersal of the population is therefore a domestic strategic aim of the highest order; otherwise, we shall cease to exist within any borders. Judea, Samaria and the Galilee are our sole guarantee for national existence, and if we do not become the majority in the mountain areas, we shall not rule in the country and we shall be like the Crusaders, who lost this country which was not theirs anyhow, and in which they were foreigners to begin with. Rebalancing the country demographically, strategically and economically is the highest and most central aim today."[179]

[Today, the Palestinians within Israeli territorial control—those in the Gaza Strip, the West Bank and the pre-1967 territorial colonization—number approximately 2.5 million. There are approximately 5.4 million Palestinians today. More than half of the Palestinian people are dispersed and scattered in a Diaspora across the world. A significant number are in the countries of the Arab East, where they are also subjected to every form of persecution and discrimination: 37.8% in Syria, Jordan and Lebanon; and 17.5% in other Arab states.]

The question posed is how to achieve the expulsion of the Palestinian people under Israeli control, particularly as Israel's entire regional strategy depends upon it: "Realizing our aims on the Eastern front depends first on the realization of this internal strategic objective."[180]

Jordan: The Short Run

The method by which this is to be accomplished requires a delicate operation, which begins to explain Zionist and American stress on Jordanian representation of the Palestinians.

"Jordan constitutes an immediate strategic target in the short run but not in the long run, for it does not constitute a real threat in the long run after its dissolution, the termination of the lengthy rule of King Hussein and the transfer of power to the Palestinians *in the short run*. [emphasis added]

"There is no chance that Jordan will continue to exist in its present structure for a long time and Israel's policy, both in war and in peace, ought to be directed at the liquidation of Jordan under the present regime and the transfer of power to the Palestinian majority."[181]

A desert land with small resources, largely dependent on Saudi money and both U.S. and Israeli military protection, Jordan's Hashemite Monarchy is scarcely sovereign at all. Its rule over the Palestinian majority who inhabit camps even as they make up its civil service, is Draconian. Palestinians have no right to political expression and when deported from the West Bank and Gaza by Israel, they are summoned daily by Jordanian police who harrass and abuse them.

The removal of the Hashemite regime is to be accompanied by what Jabotinsky, citing Hitler in 1940, euphemistically had called "population transfer."

"Changing the regime east of the river will also cause the termination of the problem of the territories densely populated with Arabs west of the Jordan [River]. Whether in war or under conditions of peace, emigration from the territories and economic demographic freeze in them, are the guarantees for the coming change on both banks of the river, and we ought to be active in order to accelerate this process in the nearest future.

"The autonomy plan ought also to be rejected, as well as any compromise or division of the territories for ... it is not possible to go on living in this country in the present situation without separating the two nations, the Arabs to Jordan and the Jews to the areas west of the river."[182]

Oded Yinon's program follows the time-honored imperial pattern of "divide and rule." Lebanon, for example, was first targeted in 1919. The cover of war has been a prerequisite for the consummation of these schemes, whether in the short or long term. Neo-colonialism remains the preferred method of imperial rule because occupations spread imperialism thin, as Che Guevara knew.

The Zionists, in particular, with their relatively small population and their total dependence on U.S. imperialism, can only enact their plan for Israeli dominion through neo-colonial schemes in the Arab East, and these require the support of their imperial master.

In this regard, Oded Yinon's blueprint is the application to the present and near future of the Zionist design pursued by Herzl, Weizman, Jabotinsky, Ben Gurion, and, today, by Peres and Shamir. Those who would select among them, offer Palestinians a Hobson's choice, for the political debate among the Zionist rulers centers on the means and timing of a conquering design.

When, for example, Moshe Dayan took Gaza in 1956, Ben Gurion became angry, informing Dayan, "I didn't want Gaza *with people,* but Gaza without people, the Galilee without people." Moshe Dayan, himself, told Zionist youth at a meeting in the Golan Heights in July 1968: "Our fathers had reached the frontiers recognized in the partition plan; the Six-Day War generation has managed to reach Suez, Jordan, and the Golan Heights. This is not the end. After the present cease-fire lines, there will be new ones. They will extend beyond Jordan ... to Lebanon and ... to central Syria as well."[182a]

Neo-colonial rule, however, depends, as Oded Yinon makes clear, upon the dialectical relation between military might and hired hands. Fragmenting the Arab states will proceed under the cover of war— whether a blitzkrieg attack, use of a proxy armed force or covert operations. The ultimate success requires local leaders who can be bought or ensnared.

Zionists, therefore, have given us repeatedly not only their "Mein Kampf," but the evidence that the preservation and extension of their rule depends on misleaders among the victim peoples. The "divide-and-rule" schemes of Zionism and their imperial patron are unending. If the Palestinians and the Arab masses are to withstand these plans for conquest, they will have to remove the corrupt regimes which barter popular aspiration. They will need to forge a revolutionary leadership which speaks openly about the role of these governments, is vocal about Zionist plans, and which shows determination to carry the struggle throughout the region.

The Four "No's"

Yinon's ideas are not outlandish. They are advocated by Sharon and Begin's Minister of Defense, Moshe Arens, and also by the Labor Party.

Y'ben Poret, a ranking official in the Israeli Ministry of Defense, was irritated in 1982 by pious criticisms of the expansion of settlements in the West Bank and Gaza: "It is," he declared, "time to rip away the veil of hypocrisy. In the present, as in the past, there is no Zionism, no settlement of the land, no Jewish state, without the removal of all the Arabs, without confiscation."[183]

The 1984 political platform of the Labor Party was promoted in full page ads in the two leading Israeli dailies, *Ma'ariv* and *Ha'aretz*. The ads highlighted the "Four No's:"
- No to a Palestinian state
- No negotiations with the P.L.O.
- No return to the 1967 borders
- No removal of any settlements.

The ad advocated an increase in the number of settlements on the West Bank and Gaza, their full funding and protection.

In 1985, the President of Israel, Chaim Herzog, a Labor Party leader, echoed the sentiments of Sharon and Shamir emphasized by Oded Yinon.

"We are certainly not willing to make partners of the Palestinians in any way in a land that was holy to our people for thousands of years. There can be no partner with the Jews of this land."[184]

As with Camp David, even a Bantustan on parts of the West Bank and Gaza would be but a prelude to the next "dispersal." Forcing 2.5 million Palestinians into Jordan is, another interim measure, for Israeli "lebensraum" [Hitler's infamous phrase meaning "living space"] will not be confined by the Jordan River.

"It should be clear, under any future political situation or military constellation, that the solution of the problem of the indigenous Arabs will come only when they recognize the existence of Israel in secure borders up to the Jordan River *and beyond it* [emphasis added], as our existential need in this difficult epoch, the nuclear epoch which we shall soon enter."[185]

Palestinian Population Transfer

Yinon's ideas were also echoed in an important story carried by *The Washington Post* on its front page on February 7, 1988, under the headline "Expelling Palestinians: It Isn't a New Idea and It Isn't Just Kahane's."

Two Israeli journalists, Yossi Melman, diplomatic correspondent of the Israeli daily, *Davar*, and Dan Raviv, London-based CBS News correspondent, disclosed that barely two weeks after the end of the June 1967 war, secret Israeli cabinet meetings were convened to discuss the "resettlement of Arabs." The information was obtained from private diaries kept by Ya'acov Herzog, director general of the Prime Minister's office. The official transcript of the meeting remains secret.

According to the *Post* article, Prime Minister Menachem Begin recommended the demolition of the refugee camps and the transfer of the Palestinians to the Sinai. Finance Minister Pinhas Sapir and Foreign Minister Abba Eban, both Labor Zionists, disagreed. They called for the transfer of all the refugees "to neighboring Arab countries, mainly Syria and Iraq."

The 1967 cabinet meeting did not reach a decision.

"Sentiment seemed to favor Deputy Prime Minister Yigal Allon's proposal that the Palestinians ... should be transported to the Sinai desert," the *Post* article states. Accordingly, the Prime Minister's office, the Defense Ministry and the army jointly set up a "secret unit charged with 'encouraging' the departure of the Palestinians for foreign shores."

The secret plan was revealed by Ariel Sharon before a Tel Aviv audience in November 1987, when he disclosed the existence of an "organization" which for years had transferred Palestinians to other countries, including Paraguay, with whose government Israel had made the necessary arrangements.

These "transfers" were handled by the Israeli military governor's office in Gaza. When one of the transferees, Talal ibn-Dimassi, attacked the Israeli consulate in Asunción, Paraguay, killing the Consul's secretary, complications ensued:

"The attack in Paraguay put an abrupt end to the secret Israeli plan which the government had hoped would help solve the problem of the Palestinians by exporting them," the *Post* article states.

Over one million people were contemplated for "transfer." Only 1,000 were successfully sent out.

Melman and Raviv emphasize that the relocation of Palestinians is not new "as the 1967 cabinet discussions show." They state that a similar scheme would be attractive to a growing number of Israelis "as they watch the recent uprising in the West Bank and Gaza."

An Option Long Considered

The authors acknowledge that the removal of the Palestinians has been the central focus of Zionist planning since the inception of the movement. They write:

"Since the early days of Zionism, resettlement has been an option for dealing with the problem posed by the large Arab population in the historical land of Israel."

Melman and Raviv recount a series of schemes which were designed to effect the removal of the Palestinian people. The East bank of the Jordan River [the state of Jordan] was contemplated, a scheme indicated in March 1988 in a full-page advertisement republishing a column by George Will which equates Jordan with Palestine.[185a]

Labor Zionists and Revisionists were united on the necessity to transfer the Palestinians elsewhere. Vladimir Jabotinsky spelled out the various efforts made since World War I in a letter written in November 1939:

"We should instruct American Jewry to mobilize a half billion dollars in order that Iraq and Saudi Arabia will absorb the Palestinian Arabs. There is no choice: The Arabs must make room for the Jews in Eretz Israel. If it was possible to transfer the Baltic peoples, it is also possible to move the Palestinian Arabs."

By 1947, Labor Zionists and Revisionists joined together in the mass expulsion of 800,000 Palestinians. In 1964, a young Israeli colonel named Ariel Sharon instructed his staff to determine "the number of buses, vans and trucks required in case of war to transport ... the Arabs out of northern Israel."

In 1967, Israeli military commanders began the process.

"One general sent bulldozers to demolish three Arab villages near Latrun on the road to Jerusalem, expelling their residents."

Such an expulsion order was issued for the West Bank city of Qalqilya and then cancelled.

Since the Uprising began in December 1987, Michael Dekel of the Likud has taken up the call "to transfer the Arabs," and Gideon Patt, a government minister from the Liberal Party, has declared that the Palestinians should be placed on trucks and sent to the border.

Melman and Raviv conclude with the following prognosis:

"Kahane's message—expel the Palestinians or risk losing control of the land of Israel—remains a potent one. And in the absence of a political solution to the Palestinian problem [sic], Israel may be pushed toward desperate measures."

A Warning by Sharon

It is in this context that Ariel Sharon's declaration of March 24, 1988, is to be assessed. Sharon stated that if the Palestinian uprising continued, Israel would have to make war on its Arab neighbors. The war, he stated, would provide "the circumstances" for the removal of the entire Palestinian population from inside Israel and from the West Bank and Gaza.

That these are not idle remarks or restricted to Sharon became clear when Yossi Ben Aharon, director general of the office of the Prime Minister, declared in Los Angeles:

"Israel has acquired a reputation of not waiting until a potential danger becomes actual."

Ben Aharon was referring to the acquisition by Saudi Arabia of silkworm missiles from China intended to menace Iran. The Israeli declaration was taken very seriously by the Saudis, President Mubarak of Egypt and the Reagan administration, inducing a "flurry of diplomatic activity."

The March 23, 1988, *New York Times* reports:

"The Reagan administration has expressed its concern that Israel not conduct any pre-emptive attack on Chinese-built missiles purchased recently by Saudi Arabia. ... Israel has not given a definitive reply to the Administration's appeals to refrain from attacking the Saudi missiles. The missiles ... were discussed during Mr. Shamir's visit to Washington last week."

Within two days of Ben Aharon's statement, Hosni Mubarak warned Israel that Egypt "would react to an Israeli attack on Saudi Arabia's new medium-range missile sites as 'firmly and decisively' as if it were an attack on Egypt itself."[185b]

This statement was followed by Mubarak with a second declaration in what was described as "a deepening crisis."

"Mubarak told reporters that he took a 'grave' view of reports that Israel was considering a preemptive air strike to destroy the missiles. ... 'This is a grave, grave matter. An Israeli attack ... would blow up the entire peace process. I warn against any attack on Saudi Arabia which is a sisterly and friendly country.'"[185b]

These public responses by President Mubarak indicate that the possibility of an Israeli adventure, intended to provide cover for expulsion of the Palestinians and to fragment Saudi Arabia, the paymaster of the Arab regimes, is not an idle one.

The timing of *The Washington Post* story of February 7, 1988, may be more than fortuitous. The Israeli authorities have no answer to the uprising of the Palestinian people other than intensified repression.

Israel and U.S. Power

If the Palestinian people face the destruction of their organized existence by Israel, one fact must be stressed: The Zionist state is nothing but the extension of the power of the United States in the region. Israeli extermination plans, occupations and expansion are on behalf of the principal imperialist power in the world.

Whatever may be the tactical divergences which emerge from time to time between Israel and the United States, there is no Zionist campaign that can sustain itself without the backing of its principal sponsor. The U.S. government between 1949 and 1983, provided $92.2 billion in military aid, economic aid, loans, special grants and tax deductible "bonds and gifts."[186]

As Joseph C. Harsh, put it in the August 5, 1982, issue of *The Christian Science Monitor:*

"Few countries in history have been as dependent on another as Israel is on the United States. Israel's major weapons are from the United States—either as gifts or on long-term, low-interest loans, which few seriously expect to be repaid.

"Israel's survival is underwritten and subsidized from Washington. Without American arms, Israel would lose the quantitative and qualitative advantage which President Reagan has promised to maintain for them. Without the economic subsidy, Israel's credit would vanish and its economy would collapse.

"In other words, Israel can only do what Washington allows it to do. It dare not conduct a single military operation without the tacit consent of Washington. When it does undertake a military offensive, the world assumes correctly that it has Washington's tacit consent."

The Israeli state is not coextensive with the Jews as a people. Zionism, historically, has been a minority ideology among Jews. A state is but an apparatus which enforces specific economic and social relations. It is a structure of power and its purpose is, however guised, to coerce and to impose obedience.

If, for example, the apartheid state of South Africa had three-fifths less territory or two-thirds less people under its control, it would not be a whit less unjust. An oppressive state is unacceptable whether it presides over a postage stamp or a continent. The Namphy regime in Haiti is no less repugnant because of the relatively small size of that country or of the population over which it rules.

Our attitude toward a state which exploits and demeans its subjects is not conditioned by the extent of its sovereign reach. We know this to be true for Stroessner's Paraguay or Zhvikov's Bulgaria. It is no less true of the Zionist state of Israel.

Even if the apartheid Israeli state were anchored on a ship off of Haifa, it would be an outrage. Like the South African state, Pinochet's Chile or the state in America (run by 2% of the population who control 90% of the national wealth), we owe it no allegiance.

Blood, Sweat and Tears

Nearly fifty years ago, an orator responded not to the occupation of his country or the liquidation of three-fourths of its towns and villages. He was not reacting to massacre, mass imprisonment, detention camps and torture. He did not decry the theft of the land and property of an entire people or their overnight transformation into pauperized refugees existing in tent camps, hunted and persecuted wherever they fled. He did not denounce a forty-year ordeal punctuated by unrelenting bombing, invasion and yet further dispersal. He responded to but a few weeks of sporadic bombing as he declaimed, memorably:

"I have nothing to offer you but blood, tears, and sweat. You ask, 'What is our policy?' I say it is to wage war, by sea, land and air. With all our might and with all the strength that God can give us to wage war against a monstrous tyranny, never surpassed in the dark, lamentable catalog of human crime. That is our policy.

"You ask, 'What is our aim?' I answer in one word—victory. Victory at all costs. Victory in spite of all terror. Victory however long and hard the road may be. For without victory for us, there is no survival, let that be realized, no survival. I feel sure that our cause will not be subject to failure and I feel entitled to claim the aid of all."

And a week later, he declared:

"We shall defend our island, whatever the cost may be. We shall fight on the beaches. We shall fight on the landing grounds. We shall fight in the fields. We shall fight in the streets. We shall fight in the hills. We shall never surrender. And even if, which I do not for a moment believe, this island were subjugated and starving, we shall carry on the struggle."

What is it that makes it permissible for the head of the Raj, the Imperial Raj, Winston Churchill, to utter these sentiments—but renders them illicit for the Palestinian people? Nothing, but that endemic racism which colors consciousness in our society.

Winston Churchill was a belligerent spokesperson of British imperialism, notably in Palestine and the Arab world. If Churchill can be allowed, demagogically, to sound a call to resist aggression and attack, how much more are the Palestinian people entitled to fight back—to resist occupation, to battle for their survival and social justice.

CHAPTER THIRTEEN

A Strategy for Revolution

There are over five million settlers of European origin in South Africa. The Afrikaaner population and those of British descent have lived in South Africa for many generations. Yet very few people, let alone those purporting to be advocates of self-determination for Blacks in South Africa, propose two states—a European white state with guaranteed security alongside a demilitarized African state.

In fact, it is precisely the existence of such an arrangement in the form of the Bantustans in South Africa which has rendered utterly indefensible this cover for the preservation of racist rule.

Similarly, in colonial Algeria and in Northern and Southern Rhodesia, the large European settler populations—many of them descendants of generations of settlers—were not accorded a separate status, let alone a settler state on usurped land of the oppressed.

On the contrary, in South Africa—as in Algeria, Zambia or Zimbabwe—it is understood that self-determination of a colonized people cannot be equated with a settler state. It is sleight of hand to suggest that, having dispossessed the population by force, the settlers now have an equivalent claim to the conquered territory.

If this is universally understood elsewhere, why this indecent exceptionalism when it comes to Israel?

Those who would foist upon the Palestinian people the demand that they recognize an apartheid Israeli state know full well that the national rights of a colonized people do not extend to their colonizers.

In Israel, no less than in South Africa, minimum justice requires dismantling the apartheid state and replacing it with a democratic secular Palestine, where citizenship and rights are not determined by ethnic criteria.

In reality, the supposed supporters of Palestinian human rights who urge acceptance and recognition of the Israeli state are, however disguised, acting as lawyers for the colonial state in Palestine. Their advocacy carries the pseudo-left cover of self-determination for "both" peoples, but this specious employment of the principle of self-determination translates into a covert call for amnesty for Israel.

Many so-called realists argue that Palestinian acknowledgment of the "right" of apartheid Israel to exist will hasten the day when a Palestinian state would be permitted by the Zionists to come into being. But this rationalization does not carry much conviction. The Zionists do not depend upon verbal acceptance for their state, but upon armed force.

For Palestinians to accept, recognize and thereby legitimize the murderous conquest of their land would merely permit the Zionists to contend that forty years of intransigence on the part of the oppressed are responsible for their suffering. It would sanction the claim that Israel was a legitimate construct from the start.

Rather than acting as a bridge toward the establishment of a unitary Palestine, as some in the P.L.O. leadership contend today, the establishment of a "mini-state" on the West Bank—and the recognition of the Zionist state, which is a pre-condition for its creation—would represent a giant obstacle in its path.

Recognition of the Israeli state would invalidate retroactively the right of resistance of the oppressed and would provide cover for the Zionist demand that only Palestinians who had capitulated and sanctioned Israel in the past, accepting its legitimacy, have the right to negotiate with Israel. When you dance with the Devil, your speech reveals his breath.

What of the Palestinians who live inside the 1967 borders, and what of the Jews themselves? Would apartheid end in South Africa, or the state be transformed by recognizing its right to exist? Would we serve the interests of the people of Paraguay or Chile by accepting the claims to legitimacy of Stroessner or Pinochet, or by providing sanction for the states they have constructed?

International Peace Conference

Despite the obvious answers to all these questions, there are, nonetheless, an increasing number of people who, today, are actively pushing for an international peace conference on the Middle East with the goal of establishing a Palestinian "mini-state" alongside the Israeli state.

On January 10, 1988, for example, *Al-Fajr*, a Jerusalem Palestinian weekly, published a statement signed by prominent Jews and Arabs which called for "a peaceful resolution of the Israeli-Palestinian conflict" that would "ensure both Israeli and Palestinian national rights."

In an interview with the Reuters press service on January 18, Hanna Siniora, editor of *Al Fajr*, specified how Israeli and Palestinian "national rights" might be ensured at such an international peace conference. Siniora called for "an association among Israel, Jordan, and a Palestinian state like that of the Benelux countries—with a demilitarized West Bank as the Luxemburg."

"Palestinians, including Arafat, would accept autonomy as an interim step toward independence," Siniora said. "Autonomy is a step that would lead eventually to negotiations between the state of Israel and the P.L.O., ending in a Palestinian state emerging as a result of those negotiations."

Siniora met with Secretary of State George Shultz in Washington on January 28 to discuss this proposal. Siniora's meeting occurred only days after P.L.O. Chairman Yasir Arafat had announced that he was interested in making a deal with Israel and the United States. A dispatch from Associated Press on January 17 explained Arafat's overtures: "Arafat says that if those countries [Israel and the United States] agree to an international conference on Middle East peace, he will recognize Israel's right to exist. The White House says this could be an encouraging sign...."

A "Rump" Palestinian State

George Ball, who served as Under Secretary of State under the Kennedy and Johnson administrations, spelled out how the United States and Israel should approach an international peace conference. Ball's article, which is titled "Peace for Israel hinges on a state for Palestinians," states the following:

"Israel's security worries could be largely met by writing stringent, enforceable safeguards into a formal treaty, denying the new [Palestinian] state any armed force of its own and limiting the numbers and kinds of weapons available to its police.

"As a further safeguard, the settlement could require installation of surveillance posts larger and more numerous and effective than those now functioning in the Sinai under Israel's peace agreement with Egypt."[186a]

Ball explains that the establishment of what he openly admits would be a "rump Palestinian state in the West Bank" is a matter of urgency. "If the United States does not seriously seek to bring the parties together," Ball warns, "the ... warfare in the Holyland will spread and intensify; sooner or later, the neighboring Arab states—even Egypt—will be dragged into the maelstrom."

The "maelstrom" that this imperialist spokesperson so strongly fears is the emancipation of the Arab masses of the region from the Israeli colonial-settler state; from the feudal sheiks of the Gulf and Arabian peninsula; and from the Egyptian regime, which has reduced the workers and peasants of Egypt to a level of poverty unknown even under King Farouk.

An international conference designed to legitimize the security interests of apartheid Israel in exchange for a Palestinian "Bantustan" can never be viable except if a Palestinian leadership were to provide this plan with protective coloration. Such an outcome will merely hand to the P.L.O. the unenviable task of policing the Palestinian people and of converting self-determination into another sad replica of the country-selling regimes which plague the Arab masses—from Jordan to Syria and from Egypt to the Gulf.

It was but a few years ago that no Palestinian nationalist would dare associate him or herself with so blatant an effort to betray the long years of struggle for Palestinian self-determination and emancipation, let alone translate the Palestinian cause into a plea for a role in preserving the status quo in the region—with its grinding poverty and relentless exploitation and subordination to U.S. imperialist control.

Those who argue that it is practical to propose a two-state solution because this plan is more likely to be accepted are guilty, decency aside, of what C. Wright Mills called "crackpot realism."

There has never been any component of the Zionist movement—from its nominal "right" to its self-designated "left"—which has accepted Palestinian statehood in any form compatible with self-determination.

A revealing example of the dangers for the Palestinian revolution of a "mini-state" proposal comes from the pen of Jerome M. Segal, a research scholar at the University of Maryland and a founder of the Jewish Committee for Israeli-Palestinian Peace.

Segal, who represents the "left" wing of the Zionist movement, writes the following in a February 16, 1988, *Los Angeles Times* article titled, "A Palestinian state serves interests of Israelis, too:"

"Ironically, of all the alternatives an independent Palestinian state in the West Bank and Gaza is the one solution that best serves Israeli security....

"A Palestinian state would be the fullest possible satisfaction of the demands of Palestinian nationalism. ... It would win the support of the P.L.O. and is the only likely basis on which the P.L.O. would formally abandon the right to return to the land and villages lost in 1948. As the recognized embodiment of the Palestinian cause, only the P.L.O. can compromise in the name of the Palestinians....

"A Palestinian state would be a demilitarized mini-state. It would be completely enclosed by Israel on one side and Jordan on the other. No military supplies or forces could reach it without passing through Israel or Jordan.

"The foreign policy of such a mini-state would be dominated by its links to the Israeli economy and by its national-security realities. In the event of a war, its very existence would be in jeopardy. ... Israel would not be seriously threatened if hostilities broke out....

"For Israel, a Palestinian state is not a charming prospect. It is simply better than the alternatives."

Segal's call for what amounts to a "rump Palestinian state in the West Bank" is a mockery of Palestinian self-determination.

Indeed, far from being willing to relinquish control of the West Bank and Gaza, the Zionists—as Ben Gurion, Dayan and Oded Yinon make clear—are too busy plotting the conquest of Kuwait.

The day that African or Palestinian rights are secured with the sanction of apartheid South Africa or by Zionist Israel under U.S. control will be the day we learn that Caligula was a disciple of Jesus, Hitler embraced Marx, and Bull Conner, eyes rolled to Heaven, chanted, "We shall overcome."

Meanwhile, the tortured, the dying, the oppressed cannot afford the fantasies of their "practical" reformist friends; the price of such illusions is paid in blood. The "rump Palestinian state" of George Ball's vision will be operated for the privileged on the backs of the Palestinian poor. Those Palestinian leaders who embrace this concocted entity—modeled on the inspiring examples of the dependent sheikdoms of the Gulf and the Bantustans of South Africa—will become the Chiang Kai-sheks, Tshombes, and King Husseins of suffering Palestine. The rights of the Palestinian people can never be advanced in this way.

For a Democratic Secular Palestine

In 1968, twenty years after the colonial-settler state of Israel was established, the Palestinian resistance movement formulated its demand for self-determination in the call for the replacement of the Israeli state with an independent, unitary Palestine.

The majority wing of the Palestine Liberation Organization, Fatah, set forth the program for the establishment of a "democratic, secular Palestine." This slogan called for the dismantling of the Zionist Israeli state and the establishment of a new state in Palestine in which Jews, Christians, and Arabs would live as equals without discrimination.

What was notable about this brave proposal was that (1) it categorically rejected any accommodation with or recognition of the Zionist state; and (2) it rejected the proposal for a Palestinian "mini-state" on the West Bank and Gaza.

P.L.O. Chairman Yasir Arafat described his proposal as follows in a remarkable biography written by journalist Alan Hart:

"We were saying 'no' to the Zionist state, but we were saying 'yes' to the Jewish people of Palestine. To them we were saying, 'You are welcome to live in our land, but on one condition—You must be prepared to live among us as equals, not as dominators.'

"I myself have always said that there is only one guarantee for the safety and security of the Jewish people in Palestine—and that is the friendship of the Arabs among whom they live."[187]

A document submitted by Arafat's Fatah organization to the Second World Congress on Palestine in September 1970 spells out the profile of a democratic and secular Palestine even more clearly. The 1970 Fatah document states:

"Pre-1948 Palestine—as defined during the British mandate—is the territory to be liberated. ... It should be quite obvious at this stage that the new Palestine discussed here is not the occupied West Bank or the Gaza Strip or both. These are areas occupied by the Israelis since June 1967. The homeland of the Palestinians usurped and colonized in 1948 is no less dear or important than the part occupied in 1967.

"Besides, the very existence of the racist oppressor state of Israel, based on the expulsion and forced exile of part of its citizens, even from one tiny village, is unacceptable to the revolution. Any arrangement accommodating the aggressor settler state is unacceptable and temporary....

"All the Jews, Moslems, and Christians living in Palestine or forcibly exiled from it will have the right to Palestinian citizenship. ... This means that all Jewish Palestinians—at the present Israelis—have the same rights provided, of course, that they reject Zionist racist chauvinism and fully agree to live as Palestinians in the new Palestine. ... It is the belief of the revolution that the majority of the present Israeli Jews will change their attitudes and will subscribe to the new Palestine, especially after the oligarchic state machinery, economy, and military establishment are destroyed."[188]

Role of Soviet Bureaucracy

The Soviet bureaucracy reacted sharply to Fatah's attempt to transform the P.L.O. into a revolutionary movement with a program and strategy aimed at mobilizing the masses and winning them for a revolutionary transformation of a settler regime.

According to Alan Hart, whose biography of Arafat was "written in cooperation with Yasir Arafat and the top leadership of the P.L.O.," the Soviet leaders told Arafat that they were fully committed to the existence of the state of Israel and that they had not the slightest intention of supporting or encouraging Palestinian militance or military capacity.[189]

Two of Fatah's principal leaders, Khalid al-Hassan and Khalil al-Wazir (Abu Jihad), went to Moscow to explain Fatah's program. They left Moscow, to cite Khalid al-Hassan, "With the clear impression that the Palestinians would not receive Soviet support for their cause until they were ready to accept Israel's existence inside the borders as they were on the eve of the [June 1967] Six Day War."[190]

"Because we were ourselves beginning to be educated about the reality of international politics," reflects Hani al-Hassan, Khalid's brother, "we realized that we couldn't expect to advance our cause without the support of at least one of two superpowers. We had knocked on the door of the United States and its Western allies and we had received no answer, so we wanted to try with the Soviets. We had no choice."[191]

Retreat to "Mini-State" Position

Fatah's leaders soon lost all confidence in the possibility of sustaining the political program which they had once proclaimed—that of a democratic and secular Palestine for which they had planned to struggle by mobilizing the Palestinian and Jewish masses.

In February 1974, a P.L.O. working paper was formulated which retreated from this program. The paper proposed "To establish a national authority on any lands that can be wrested from Zionist occupation."[192]

Arafat and the majority of his Fatah colleagues were now committed to working for a negotiated "settlement" which required the Palestinian people to accept the loss "for all time" of 70% of their original homeland in exchange for a "mini-state" on the West Bank and Gaza.

Arafat openly acknowledged that the entire Palestinian people were opposed to this policy. Alan Hart writes:

"Arafat and most of his senior colleagues in the leadership knew they needed time to sell it to the rank and file of the liberation movement. If, in 1974, Arafat and his colleagues had openly admitted the true extent of the compromise they were prepared to make, *they would have been repudiated and rejected by an easy majority of the Palestinians.*"[193] [emphasis added]

Arafat was now embarked upon a course in which he could not tell the truth to his own people about the political line which he and his colleagues had taken. The words are those of Yasir Arafat:

"Our tragedy at the time was that the world refused to understand there were two aspects, two sides, to the question of what was possible. First, there was the question of what it was possible for the Palestinians to achieve in practical terms—given the fact that the *two* [emphasis added] superpowers were committed to Israel's existence....

"But there was also the question of what it was possible for the Palestinian leadership to persuade its people to accept. When a people is claiming the return of 100% of its land, it's not so easy for leadership to say, 'No, you can take only 30%.'"[194]

The disparity between the public posture and the private practice became the touchstone of P.L.O. political practice in this period, with considerable confusion and demoralization among the masses arising from it. Arafat is frank about this:

"You say to me and you are right, that our public position on the compromise we were prepared to make was ambiguous for many years while we were educating our people about the need for compromise. But I must also tell you that our real position was always known to the governments of the world, including the government of Israel.

"How? From 1974, even from the end of 1973, certain of our people were officially authorized to maintain secret contacts with Israelis and with important people in the West. Their responsibility was *to say in secret what at the time we could not say in public.*"[195] [emphasis added]

This clandestine policy was carried out for five years, from 1974 to 1979, with neither awareness nor endorsement by the elected members of the Palestine National Council. It required diplomatic maneuvering and lobbying.

It also required, to quote Alan Hart, "out-maneuvering and outwitting those [in the P.L.O. "left"] who were opposed to the 'mini-state.'" Hart explains:

"If he had been put to the test of actual negotiations by Israel between 1974 and 1979 ... Arafat could not have delivered peace on the basis of the 'mini-state' formula without splitting the P.L.O."[196]

But inducing the "left" to acquiesce proved to be like pushing on an open door. And by the time of the 1979 Palestine National Congress, George Habash and the Popular Front for the Liberation of Palestine (PFLP) had endorsed the "mini-state" plan. Indeed, by 1979, all components of the P.L.O. had adopted the call for a "mini-state" on the West Bank and Gaza. From 1974 on, all wings of the P.L.O. had demonstrated they were incapable of formulating an independent, revolutionary strategy for the Palestinian struggle.

Addressing the Jewish Working Class

As the 1970 Fatah document correctly noted, the future of the struggle of the Palestinian people is tied up with a political strategy which addresses itself to Israeli Jews and which calls upon them to join with the Palestinians in a struggle for a democratic and secular Palestine.

Indeed, within the Zionist state, 68% of the settler population is made up of Oriental (mainly Sephardic) Jews. They come from countries which are impoverished, many of them often with retrograde regimes.

The great mass of Oriental Jews are poor. So the means which are used to keep them down economically and politically, are the same used in any ghetto, barrio or working-class neighborhood across the United States or anywhere else.

The Oriental Jews *do* have the same rights under Israeli law—in formal terms. Here's the problem: In Israel, after the 9th grade, there are special charges which make a high-school education very costly. This means, in practice, that only a tiny percentage of Oriental Jews go on to obtain a higher education. Oriental Jews comprise 10% of university students and 3% of university graduates. This follows from economic exploitation.

Their political representation does not reflect their proportion of the population. Oriental Jews hold only one sixth of the seats in the Knesset [Israel's Parliament]. Elie Eliachar, a prominent leader of the Oriental community and a former member of the Knesset, explained that even this representation is nominal. In effect, the Oriental deputies represent "all-Ashkenazi political parties to which they owe sole allegiance rather than the Sephardi-Oriental community." "This," he writes, "makes Israeli democracy a mere caricature."[197]

There should, however, be no misunderstanding. The Oriental Jews are very often Zionist. It would be misleading to talk about them without making it clear that the Israelis, like all imperialist and colonial powers, have used the divide-and-rule approach in handling them.

The Oriental Jews have a very precarious socio-economic status in Israel. They are but slightly better off than the Palestinians themselves. A Jew from Iraq, Morocco, or Yemen, moreover, is an Arab of Jewish religious orgins. In mores, manner, custom, and appearance, they are as their Moslem and Christian brothers and sisters. They also suffer discrimination. The Zionists continually attempt to instill racist hatred in the Oriental Jews for the Palestinian masses.

When young Oriental Jews are sent to fight in Lebanon or to the West Bank and Gaza, their eyes are opened to Israel's war policies. They come back to the same miserable economic and social position they endured before they left. This was what had led in years past to the development of a Black Panther movement in the Sephardic slums and to the beginnings of a radicalization among the Sephardim. There is a rage barely beneath the surface, and one of these days the explosion will happen within the Sephardic community. This is inevitable.

When the Palestinian people begin to mobilize it cannot but speak to the condition of the Jewish working class. It behooves a Palestinian revolutionary leadership to address the Jews with a vision of a democratic-secular Palestine. In time, the Jewish workers will respond to Palestinian mobilization. The first step is to think, "If they can do it, so can we." The second is to look around for allies. That is the road to an anti-Zionist revolutionary movement.

Crisis of Revolutionary Leadership

Despite the tremendous revolutionary opportunities over the past several years, the leadership of the P.L.O. has shown itself unable to develop a strategy for the mobilization in Palestine of the Palestinian and Jewish masses against the Zionist state.

Neither the "moderate" leadership of Yasir Arafat, the "progressive" leadership of the Popular and Democratic Fronts, nor the "dissident" Fatah rebels have formulated a strategy for the Palestinian people independent of the rotten capitalist regimes of the region.

The P.L.O. leaders at one moment curry favor with imperialism and its agents, the country-selling regimes of the Arab East, and at another indulge in random acts of force. Each course is designed, misguidedly, to induce imperialism to endorse the establishment of a Palestinian "mini-state."

But these regimes—from Syria to Jordan to Egypt—regard the Palestinian revolution as a clear and present danger. They understand that the extraordinary struggle of the Palestinian nation—even under the nationalist P.L.O. leadership—is a reminder to their own suffering people of what is to be done and who is in the way.

A revolutionary Palestinian leadership should struggle, as many do, for the dismantlement of the Israeli state.

The assassination of Khalil al-Wazir (Abu Jihad) on April 17, 1988, was a clear message to the Fatah wing of the P.L.O. and to the Arab governments. It is virtually impossible, now, for this leadership to project plausibly a "settlement" with Israel. Their expectations of negotiations which could result in some limited form of Palestinian self-determination have been shown to be illusory. The Israeli intent was to prompt an armed response from within the uprising; indeed, a staged provocation by Israeli intelligence in the name of the Intifadeh is not precluded. For the basic Zionist agenda is to depopulate Palestine, and the cover of war is needed to effect yet again a mass expulsion of Palestinians.

The Israeli press unanimously ascribed the murder operation to Israeli Navy commando units and the Mossad, an assault involving thirty people. *Davar* reported on April 18 that the decision to assassinate Abu Jihad was approved at the cabinet level while Secretary of State George Shultz was in Jerusalem and proceeded after receiving a green light from the United States.

The *Davar* editorial confirms that the assassination is to be "credited to ministers Shamir, Rabin and Peres."[198] Davar reported that Prime Minister Yitzhak Shamir "leapt with joy" upon hearing the news and sent congratulatory telegrams to each of the perpetrators. Shamir had carried out such murders of his own in the past, notably of

United Nations mediator Count Folke Bernadotte on September 17, 1948. Such an operation, with all its implications, could not occur without U.S. sanction. It reveals the real nature of the Shultz "peace" proposals. They are a cover for preparations to crush the uprising and for a new war.

The tragic death of Abu Jihad is particularly instructive in its timing. The Mossad has had the ability to murder major figures, such as Abu Jihad, in the past. His killing is the equivalent of a declaration of war. It underlines, once again, the necessity for a new strategy on the part of a revolutionary Palestinian leadership, one based on a political program directed to the Palestinian and Jewish masses for the replacement of the Zionist state.

The Way Forward

The Palestinian masses are in motion. The extraordinary will to struggle on the part of the entire population has shown that there is no going back. The Intifadeh needs to focus on specific features of oppression and to challenge them by reclaiming the land, planting forbidden crops, sinking wells and withholding labor in the course of demanding unconditional Israeli withdrawal.

A revolutionary Palestinian leadership will need to devise a program for inside the Green Line which addresses the Jews within Israel as well as the Moslems and Christians. In short, what is necessary is a blueprint for a post-Zionist society which inspires people and associates the inequities of their lives with the Zionist state.

As the Zionist state is at once a species of capitalist class rule and an extension of U.S. imperial power in the region, the struggle against Zionism becomes, programmatically, a struggle for a socialist Palestine and, as the dawn follows the long night, a struggle for a socialist Arab East—from the Mediterranean to the Gulf.

A P.L.O. faithful to its promise of a democratic-secular Palestine would include in its leadership those anti-Zionist Jews who have fought the colonial-settler state. In this way, the Jewish masses themselves would be able to see who really speaks for them, and who offers them a way out of perpetual war, insecurity, and deprivation.

A clear call for a democratic and secular Palestine is essential to uniting mass social forces capable of dismantling the Zionist state and replacing it with a humane society dedicated to the ending of class and national oppression.

The Palestinian revolutionary movement can only advance by hammering out a new strategy based on combining the Palestinian national struggle with the struggle of the workers and peasants of the whole Middle East for liberation from both capitalist and imperialist domination—for a socialist Middle East.

There is no short cut to liberation, as the century-old ordeal of the Palestinian people has shown. The road to victory will only be shortened when a leadership arises which knows its direction and proposes the path in a language which enlists the people, mobilizes them in their own behalf, and exposes fearlessly the false leaders dangerously in the way.

The Palestinian answer to the Zionist and imperialist schemes can be found in the stone-throwing children of Jabaliya, the Beach Camp, Balata and Dheisheh. For this, as Jabotinsky was obliged by them to acknowledge, is a people, a living people—not a rabble, but a conscious people fighting with stones and sling shots against the fourth largest military power in the world.

We owe them, at the very least, fidelity to their revolutionary struggle, which can never be complete until it extends from the Mediterranean to the Persian Gulf, from the Brook of Egypt to the Euphrates—and, as their Zionist oppressors forever proclaim, "and beyond."

The Israel of Theodore Herzl (1904) and Rabbi Fischmann (1947)

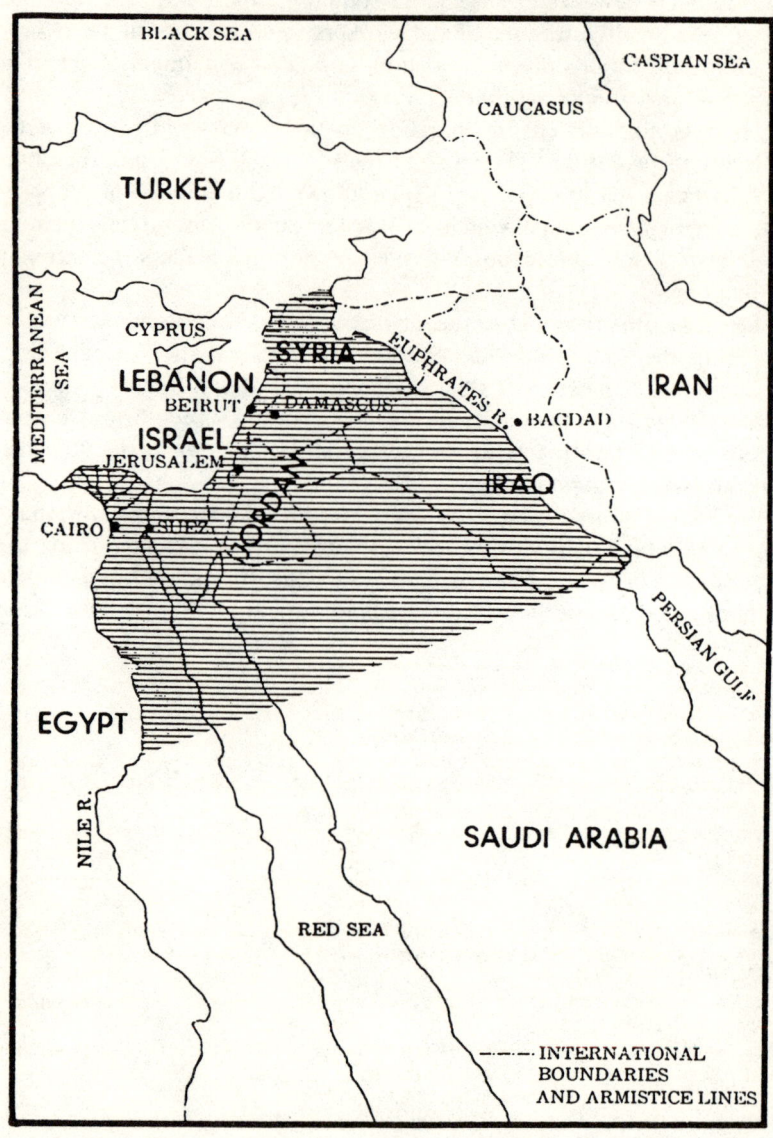

In his *Complete Diaries*, Vol. II, page 711, Theodor Herzl, the founder of Zionism, says that the area of the Jewish state stretches: "From the Brook of Egypt to the Euphrates."

Rabbi Fischmann, member of the Jewish Agency for Palestine, declared in his testimony to the U.N. Special Committee of Enquiry on July 9, 1947: "The Promised Land extends from the River of Egypt up to the Euphrates. It includes parts of Syria and Lebanon."

Footnotes

1-Dan Fisher, *Los Angeles Times*, December 20, 1987.
2-Ibid.
3-John Kifner, *New York Times*, December 22, 1987.
4-*San Francisco Examiner*, December 23, 1987.
5-First hand account to the author from Dheisheh camp.
6-Dan Fisher, *Los Angeles Times*, December 20, 1987.
7-John Kifner, *New York Times*, December 21, 1987.
8-Dan Fisher, *Los Angeles Times*, December 23, 1987.
9-Dan Fisher, *Los Angeles Times*, December 20, 1987.
10-*New York Times*, January 21, 1988.
11-John Kifner, *New York Times*, January 23, 1988.
12-John Kifner, *New York Times*, January 27, 1988.
13-Ibid.
13a-Bassam Shaka'a: Telephone conversations with the author from February 5, 1988, through March 13, 1988.
13b-John Kifner, *New York Times*, April 4 and April 15, 1988.
13c-Newsweek, "A Soldier's Account," February 8, 1988.
13d-*New York Times*, February 14, 1988.
13e-John Kifner, *New York Times*, February 21, 1988.
13f-*Los Angeles Times*, March 23, 1988.
13g-*Newsweek*, April 4, 1988.
13h-*New York Times*, April 1, 1988.
13i-*Newsweek*, March 28, 1988.
13j-Ibid.
13k-*Los Angeles Times*, March 29, 1988.
13l-*New York Times*, April 1, 1988.
13m-*The Wall Street Journal*, April 8, 1988.
14-Walter Laqueur, *History of Zionism* (London, 1972).
15-Joy Bonds et. al., *Our Roots Are Still Alive—The Story of the Palestinian People*, (New York: Institute for Independent Social Journalism, Peoples Press, 1977), p. 13.
16-Theodor Herzl, *The Jewish State* (London: 1896).
17-Hyman Lumer, *Zionism: Its Role in World Politics*, (New York: International Publishers, 1973).
18-Chaim Weizmann, *Trial and Error: The Autobiography of Chaim Weizmann*, (New York: Harpers, 1949), p. 149.
19-John Norton Moore, ed., *The Arab-Israeli Conflict*, (Princeton, N.J.: The American Society of International Law, Princeton University Press, 1977), p. 885.
20-Ibid.
21-Cited in Harry N. Howard, *The King Commission: An American Inquiry in the Middle East*, (Beirut: 1963).
22-N. Kirschner, "Zionism and the Union of South Africa: Fifty Years of Friendship and Understanding," *Jewish Affairs*, South Africa, May 1960.
23-Theodor Herzl, *Diaries*, Vol. II, p. 793.
24-Theodor Herzl, *The Jewish State: An Attempt at a Modern Solution of the Jewish Question*, p. 33. Cited in Uri Davis, *Israel: An Apartheid State*, (London: Zed Books, Ltd., 1987), p. 4.
25-Ibid., p. 28.
26-"For Love and Money," in *Israel: A Survey*, Financial Mail, Johannesburg, South Africa, May 11, 1984, p. 41.
27-"The Iron Wall"—"O Zheleznoi Stene"—*Rassvet*, November 4, 1923.

28-Lenni Brenner, *The Iron Wall: Zionist Revisionism From Jabotinsky to Shamir*, (London: Zed Books, Ltd., 1984), p. 79.
29- London *Sunday Times*, September 26, 1982.
30-Jabotinsky's "Letter on Autonomy," 1904. Cited in Brenner, *The Iron Wall*, p. 29.
31-Brenner, *The Iron Wall*, p. 31.
32-Sami Hadawi, *Bitter Harvest*, (Delmar, N.Y.: The Caravan Books, 1979), pp. 43-44.
33-Ghassan Kanafani, "The 1936-1939 Revolt in Palestine," New York, Committee for a Democratic Palestine.
34-Ibid., p. 96.
35-Ibid., p. 39.
36-Ibid., p. 31.
37-Ibid.
38-Hadawi, pp. 43-44.
39-Joseph Weitz, "A Solution to the Refugee Problem," *Davar*, September 29, 1967. Cited in Uri Davis and Norton Mezvinsky, eds., *Documents from Israel, 1967-1973*, p. 21.
40-Davis, *Israel: An Apartheid State*, p. 5.
41-*Al Hamishmar* (Israeli newspaper), September 7, 1976.
42-Cited by Fouzi El-Asmar and Salih Baransi during discussions with the author, October 1983.
43-Sabri Jiryis, *The Arabs in Israel*, (New York: Monthly Review Press, 1976).
44-Gad Becker, *Yediot Ahronot*, April 13, 1983, and *The New York Times*, April 14, 1983.
45-Ibid.
46-David Ben Gurion, *Memoirs*, Volume III, p. 467.
47-Ben Gurion, from a 1937 speech cited in his *Memoirs*.
48-David Ben Gurion, "Report to the World Council of Poale Zion (the forerunner of the Labor Party), Tel Aviv, 1938. Cited by Israel Shahak, *Journal of Palestine Studies*, Spring 1981.
49-Ben Gurion in a 1938 speech.
50-Michael Bar Zohar, *Ben Gurion: A Biography*, (New York: Delacorte, 1978)
51-Ben Gurion, July 1948, as cited by Bar Zohar.
52-Brenner, *The Iron Wall*, p. 52.
53-Ibid., p. 143.
54-Meir Pa'il, *Yediot Aharanot*, April 4, 1972. Cited by David Hirst, *The Gun and the Olive Branch*,(Great Britain: Faber & Faber Ltd., 1977), pp. 126-127.
55-Jacques de Reynier, *A Jerusalem un Drapeau Flottait sur La Ligne de Feu*, pp. 71-76. Cited by Hirst, pp. 127-8.
56-*Davar*, June 9, 1979.
57-Eldad, "On the Spirit That Was Revealed in the People," *De'ot*, Winter 1968. Davis and Mezvinsky, pp. 186-7.
58-Meir Har Tzion, *Diary*, (Tel Aviv: Levin-Epstein Ltd., 1969). Cited in Livia Rokach, *Israel's Sacred Terrorism*, (Belmont, Mass.: Association of Arab American University Graduates Inc. Press, 1980) p. 68.
59-Rokach, p. 16.
60-Ibid.
61-From the court records: *Judgments of the District Court: The Military Prosecutor vs. Malor Melinki et. al.*, Rokach, p. 66.
62-*Ha'aretz*, May 23, 1980.
63-A detailed analysis of this process can be found in Janet Abu Lughod's "The Demographic Transformation of Palestine" in Ibrahim Abu Lughod, ed., *The Transformation of Palestine*, (Evanston, Ill.: Northwestern University Press, 1971), pp. 139-64.
64- Moshe Dayan, March 19,1969, *Ha'aretz*, April 4, 1969, and cited in Davis.
65-Davis and Mezvinsky, p. 47.

66-Jewish National Fund, *Jewish Villages in Israel*, p. xxi. Quoted in Lehn and Davis, The Jewish National Fund.
67-The U.N. estimate was made in the late 1950's. Baruch Kimmerling, *Zionism and Economy*, p. 100. Cited in Davis, p. 19. In their books, Davis and Kimmerling speak of "118-120 billion Pounds Sterling." This author was unable to locate the original United Nations report, but after thorough examination of other sources, it appears Kimmerling (then Davis) made a typographical mistake. The figure should be millions of Pounds Sterling—not billions.
68-Dan Peretz, *Israel and the Palestinian Arabs*, pp. 142., Davis, pp. 20-21. South African diamonds are cut and refined in Israel, in a revealing partnership, before they are distributed to the world market.
69-Walter Lehn, "The Jewish National Fund As An Instrument of Discrimination." Cited in *Zionism and Racism*, (London: International Organization for the Elimination of All Forms of Racial Discrimination, 1977), p. 80.
69a-The Israel Lands Administration Report (Jerusalem 1962) stipulates that the I.L.A. has jurisdiction over "92.6%" of the total area of the state. Hebrew University professor Uzzi Ornan identifies the area "to which the principles of the J.N.F. apply" as "95% of pre-1967 Israel." *Ma'ariv*, January 30, 1974.
69b-Walter Lehn with Uri Davis, *The Jewish National Fund*, (London: Kegan Paul International Ltd., 1988), p. 114.
69c-Ibid., p. 115.
70-J.N.F. lease, article 23, cited in Israel Shahak, ed., *The Non-Jew in the Jewish State*, (Jerusalem: 1975)
71-*Ha'aretz*, December 13, 1974.
72- *Ma'ariv*, July 3, 1975.
73-Raphael Patai, ed., *The Complete Diaries of Theodor Herzl*, (New York: 1960), p. 88.
74-Israel Shahak, "A Message to the Human Rights Movement in America—Israel Today: The Other Apartheid," *Against the Current*, January-February 1986.
75-Ibid.
76-Marvin Lowenthal, ed., *The Diaries of Theodor Herzl*, p. 6. Cited in Lenni Brenner, *Zionism in the Age of the Dictators*, (Westport, Conn.: Lawrence Hill, 1983) p. 6.
77-From "Our Shomer 'Weltanschauung,'" Hashomer Hatzair, December 1936. Originally published in 1917, Brenner, *Zionism*, p. 22.
78-Brenner, The Iron Wall.
79-Ibid., p. 14.
80-Ibid.
81-Brenner, *Zionism*, p. 48.
82-Ibid., p. 85.
83-Ibid., p. 99.
84-Ibid., p. 149.
85-Ibid.
86-Rabbi Solomon Schonfeld, Britain's Chief Rabbi during World War II. Faris Yahya, *Zionist Relations with Nazi Germany*, (Beirut, Lebanon: Palestine Research Center, January 1978), p. 53.
87-Chaim Weizmann reporting to the Zionist Congress in 1937 on his testimony before the Peel Commission in London, July 1937. Cited in Yahya, p. 55.
88-Yitzhak Gruenbaum was chairperson of the Jewish Agency's Rescue Committee. Excerpted from a speech made in 1943. Ibid., p. 56.
89-Ibid., p. 53.
90-Ibid., pp. 59-60.
91-Ibid., p. 58.
92-Judgment given on June 22, 1955, Protocol of Criminal Case 124/53 in District Court, Jerusalem. Ibid., p. 58.

93-Ibid. p. 59.
94-Ben Hecht, *Perfidy*, (New York: 1961), pp. 58-59. Ibid., p. 60.
95-"Proposal of the National Military Organization—Irgun Zvai Leumi—Concerning the Solution of the Jewish Question in Europe and the Participation of the N.M.O. in the War on the side of Germany." Original text found in David Yisraeli, *The Palestine Problem in German Politics, 1889-1945*, (Ramat Gan, Israel: Bar Ilan University, 1974), pp. 315-317, Brenner, *Zionism*, p. 267.
96-Brenner, *The Iron Wall*, p. 107.
97-Lidice was a Czech village razed to the ground by the S.S. It became a symbol of Nazi brutality and was singled out as a war crime during the Nuremburg Trials.
98-Rokach, p. 5.
99-Ibid.
100-Ibid., p. 4.
101-Ibid., p. 6
102-Ibid., p. 14.
103-Ibid., p. 18.
104-Ibid., p. 19.
105-Ibid., p. 29
106-Ibid.
107-Ibid., p. 30.
108-Ibid., p. 55.
109-Ibid., p. 45.
110-Ibid., p. 50.
111-Herzl, *Diaries*, Vol. II, 1904, p. 711.
112-Israel Shahak, *The Zionist Plan for the Middle East*, (Belmont, Mass.: A.A.U.G., 1982).
113-Jonathan Randal, *Going All The Way*, (New York: Viking, 1983), p. 188.
114-Letter to Prime Minister Moshe Sharett, February 27, 1954. Rokach, p. 25.
115-Randal.
116-Ibid., p. 247.
117-Norwegian social worker Marianne Helle Möller, cited in Ralph Schoenman and Mya Shone, "Towards A Final Solution in the Lebanon?", *New Society*, August 19, 1982.
118-Randal.
119-Cited in a leaflet distributed in Sidon by Major Saqr, February 1983.
120-*Time Magazine*, October 4, 1982.
121-*New York Times*, October 1, 1982.
122-*Jerusalem Post*, July 23, 1982.
123-*Jerusalem Post*, October 1983.
124-Randal, p. 17.
125-Ibid.
126-Ibid.
127-Dan Fisher, *Los Angeles Times*, November 11, 1987.
128-Lea Tsemel, "Prison Conditions in Israel—An Overview," November 16, 1982, p. 1. Included in Ralph Schoenman and Mya Shone, *Prisoners of Israel: The Treatment of Palestinian Prisoners in Three Jurisdictions*, (Princeton, N.J.: Veritas Press, 1984).
129-National Lawyers Guild, *Treatment of Palestinians in Israeli-Occupied West Bank and Gaza*, (New York: 1978), p. 89.
130-London *Sunday Times*, June 19, 1977.
131-Mohammed Na'amneh, Interview with the author, East Jerusalem, February 2, 1983.
132-London *Sunday Times*, June 19, 1977, p. 18.
133-Arie Bober, ed., *The Other Israel: The Radical Case Against Zionism*, (New York: Anchor Books, 1972), p. 134.

134-Sabri Jiryis, *The Arabs In Israel*, (New York: Monthly Review Press, 1976), p. 12.
135-London *Sunday Times*, June 19, 1977.
136-Ibid., p. 18.
137-Ibid. (also the citation for the above case-studies).
138-Ibid. For Rasmiya Odeh's personal account, see also Soraya Antonius, "Prisoners for Palestine: A List of Women Political Prisoners," *Journal of Palestine Studies*.
139-Lea Tsemel, "Political Prisoners In Israel—An Overview," Jerusalem, November 16, 1982. Lea Tsemel and Walid Fahoum, "Nafha is a Political Prison," May 13, 1980, and a series of reports (May 1982—February 1983). Felicia Langer, *With My Own Eyes*, (London: Ithaca Press, 1975). Felicia Langer, *These Are My Brothers*, (London: Ithaca Press, 1979). Jamil Ala' al-Din and Melli Lerman, *Prisoners and Prisons in Israel*, (London: Ithaca Press, 1978). Walid Fahoum, two books of case histories, available in Arabic. Raja Shehadeh, *Occupier's Law: Israel and the West Bank*, (Washington, D.C.: Institute for Palestine Studies, 1985). National Lawyers Guild 1977 Middle East Delegation, *Treatment of Palestinians in Israeli-Occupied West Bank and Gaza*, (New York: 1978). Amnesty International, "Report", October 21, 1986. Ralph Schoenman and Mya Shone, *Prisoners of Israel: The Treatment of Palestinian Prisoners in Three Jurisdictions*, (Princeton, N.J.: Veritas Press, 1984) (Prepared in an abbreviated form for the United Nations International Conference on the Question of Palestine).
140-National Lawyers Guild, p. 103.
141-Case Study: Ghassan Harb, Ramallah. London *Sunday Times*, p. 19.
142-Case Study: Nader Afouri, Nablus. Schoenman and Shone, pp. 22-26.
143-Case Study: Dr. Azmi Shuaiby, El Bireh. Schoenman and Shone, pp. 30-32.
144-Case Study: Mohammed Manasrah, Bethlehem. Schoenman and Shone, pp. 33-36.
145-*Al-Fajr Jerusalem Palestinian Weekly*, March 14, 1984
146-*Al-Fajr Jerusalem Palestinian Weekly*, January 10, 1988.
147-London *Sunday Times*, p. 18.
148-Ibid.
149-Ibid.
150-American-Arab Anti-Discrimination Committee, *The Bitter Year: Arabs Under Israeli Occupation in 1982*, (Washington, D.C.: 1983), p. 211.
151-*Al-Fajr Jerusalem Palestinian Weekly*.
152-Jamil Ala' al-Din and Melli Lerman, p. 3.
153-Case Study: The Kutler Report. Ibid. pp. 34-45.
154-Lea Tsemel and Walid Fahoum, "Reports on Nafha Prison," May 1982—February 1983. Cited in Schoenman and Shone, pp. 47-54.
155-Jamil Ala' al-Din and Melli Lerman, p. 26.
156-David Ben Gurion, "Divray ha Knesset," Parliamentary Record #36, p. 217. Cited in Bober, p. 138.
157-Israel Shahak, trans. & ed., *The Zionist Plan For the Middle East*, (Belmont, Mass.: A.A.U.G., 1982)
158-Ibid., p. 5.
159-Ibid.
160-Ibid., p. 9.
161-Ibid.
162-Ibid., p. 5.
163-Ibid., p. 4.
164-Ibid., p. 5.
165-Ibid., p. 9.
166-Ibid.
167-Ibid., p. 4.
168-Ibid.
169-Ibid., p. 9.
170-Ibid., p. 5.

171-Ibid., p. 4.
172-Ibid., p. 8.
173-Ibid.
174-Ibid.
175-Ibid., p. 4.
176-Ibid., p. 4 & p. 9.
177-Ibid., p. 5.
178-Ibid., p. 10.
179-Ibid.
180-Ibid., pp. 10-11.
181-Ibid., pp. 9-10.
182-Ibid., p. 10.
182a-Sunday *London Times*, June 25, 1969.
183-*Israeli Mirror*, London.
184-Yosi Berlin, *Meichuro Shel Ichud*, 1985, p. 14.
185-Shahak, *The Zionist Plan*.
185a-*New York Times*, March 27,1988.
185b-*The Washington Post*, February 7, 1988.
185c-Ibid.
185d-Ibid.
185e-Ibid.
185f-*New York Times*, March 23, 1988.
185g-*Los Angeles Times*, March 25, 1988.
185h-Ibid.
186-For a full discussion of the financial relationship between the United States and Israel see Mohammed El Khawas & Samir Abed Rabbo, *American Aid to Israel: Nature & Impact*, (Brattleboro, Vt.: Amana Books, 1984).
186a-*Los Angeles Times*, January 17, 1988.
187-Cited in Alan Hart, *Arafat: Terrorist or Peacemaker*, (Sidgwick and Jackson, revised edition), p. 275.
188-Cited in *Documents of the Palestinian Resistance Movement*, (New York: Merit pamphlet, Pathfinder Press, 1971). The full statement by Fatah was also printed in the October 16, 1970, issue of *The Militant* newspaper.
189-Hart, p. 279.
190-Ibid., p. 277.
191-Ibid., p. 278.
192-Ibid., p. 379.
193-Ibid., p. 379
194-Ibid., p. 379.
195-Ibid., p. 379.
196-Ibid., p. 379.
197-Naseer H. Aruri, "The Oriental Jews of Israel," Zionism and Racism, p. 113.
198-*New York Times*, April 18, 1988.

Suggested Reading

Bober, Arie, ed., *The Other Israel: The Radical Case Against Zionism,* Garden City, N.Y., Anchor Books, 1972

Brenner, Lenni, *The Iron Wall: Zionist Revisionism from Jabotinsky to Shamir,* London, Zed Books, 1984

Brenner, Lenni, *Zionism in the Age of the Dictators,* Westport, Conn., Lawrence Hill, 1983

Davis, Uri, *Israel — An Apartheid State,* London, Zed Books, Ltd., 1987

El-Asmar, Fouzi, Khadr, Naim and Davis, Uri, *Towards a Socialist Republic of Palestine,* London, Ithaca Press, 1978

El-Asmar, Fouzi, *To Be An Arab In Israel,* 2nd ed., Beirut, The Institute for Palestine Studies, 1978

El-Khawas, Mohammed and Abed-Rabbo, Samir, *American Aid to Israel: Nature and Impact,* Brattleboro, Vt., Amana Books, 1984

Hadawi, Sami, *Bitter Harvest,* 4th ed., Delmar, N.Y., The Caravan Press, 1979

International Organization for the Elimination of All Forms of Racial Discrimination, ed., *Zionism and Racism,* London, 1977

Jiryis, Sabri, *The Arabs in Israel,* New York, Monthly Review Press, 1976

Kanafani, Ghassan, *The 1936-39 Revolt in Palestine,* New York, Committee for a Democratic Palestine

Lehn, Walter with Davis, Uri, *The Jewish National Fund,* London, Kegan Paul International, 1988

Palumbo, Michael, *The Palestinian Catastrophe: The 1948 Expulsion of a People from their Homeland,* London, Faber and Faber, 1987

Rodinson, Maxime, *Israel and the Arabs,* New York, Pantheon, 1968

Rodinson, Maxime, *Israel, A Colonial-Settler State?,* New York, Monad Press, 1973

Rokach, Livia, *Israel's Sacred Terrorism,* 2nd ed., Belmont, Mass., Association of Arab-American University Graduates Inc. Press, 1982

Ryan, Sheila, and Hallaj, Muhammad, *Palestine Is But Not In Jordan*, Belmont, Mass.: AAUG Inc. Press, 1983

Schoenman, Ralph and Shone, Mya, *Prisoners of Israel: The Treatment of Palestinian Prisoners in Three Jurisdictions*, Princeton, N.J., Veritas Press, 1984

Schoenman, Ralph and Shone, Mya, "Towards a Final Solution in the Lebanon," London, *New Society*, August 19, 1982

Shahak, Israel, *Israel's Global Role: Weapons for Repression*, Belmont, Mass., A.A.U.G. Inc. Press, 1982

Shahak, Israel, trans. & ed., *The Zionist Plan for the Middle East*, Belmont, Mass., A.A.U.G. Inc. Press, 1982

Shehadeh, Raja, *Occupier's Law: Israel and the West Bank*, Washington, D.C., Institute for Palestine Studies, 1985

Weinstock, Nathan, *Zionism: False Messiah*, London, Ink Links, 1979

Yayha, Faris, *Zionist Relations With Nazi Germany*, Beirut, Palestine Research Center, 1978

Zayid, Ismail, *Zionism: The Myth and the Reality*, Indianapolis, American Trust Publications, 1980

* * *

Periodicals

Al-Fajr Jerusalem Palestinian Weekly, 2025 "I" Street N.W., Washington, D.C. 20006

Israeli Mirror, 21 Collingham Rd., London SW5 ONU, U.K.

Journal of Palestine Studies, P.O. Box 19449, Washington, D.C. 20036

Palestine Perspectives, 9522A Lee Highway, Fairfax, VA 22031

The Shahak Newsletter (translations from the Israeli Press with commentary), Israel Shahak, 2 Bartenura St., Jerusalem, Israel

Socialist Action, 3435 Army St. #308, San Francisco, CA 94110

Appendix

The following is the reprinted text of a statement which first appeared in the March 13, 1988, issue of *The New York Times*. The ad was placed by the Campaign to End all Aid to Israel/For a Democratic Secular Palestine. The Campaign's executive director is Ralph Schoenman. Its coordinator is Mya Shone. The signatories had organizations and titles listed for identification purposes only.

The Time Has Come: End All Aid to Apartheid Israel

We cannot stand silently by as we watch young men and old, women and children murdered daily in cold blood — shot at point point blank range, savagely beaten unto death with heavy staves, their heads, hands and limbs smashed.

We cannot permit a ruthless state to poison people with toxic gas and bury young men alive.

We shall never accept an entire people denied the elementary democratic and human rights we insist upon for ourselves. Were we subjected to a brutal occupation, daily humiliation, military rule, mass imprisonment and institutionalized torture, we too would rise up in revolt.

The rebellion of the Palestinian people has been a long time coming. Twenty years of occupation are but one dimension of their tragedy. They were driven from their original homes, villages and land by sustained massacre, condemned to miserable camps, subjected in a far-flung Diaspora to renewed slaughter, saturation bombing and unending persecution.

The tyranny suffered in the West Bank and Gaza is but the little continuation of how all of Palestine was colonized. Between the time of the partition of Palestine in 1947 and the formation of Israel, Zionist militia seized 75% of the land and drove out 800,000 Palestinians through a series of massacres.

When the state of Israel was declared, there were 475 Palestinian cities, towns and villages. Of these, 385 were razed to the ground — disappearing from the map. The 90 remaining were denuded of land, confiscated without compensation.

Today, the Jewish National Fund administers 93% of the land of Israel. To live on land, lease it, sharecrop or work on it, one must establish four generations of maternal Jewish descent.

If, in any country, people had to prove they did **not** have generations of maternal Jewish descent in order to enjoy elementary rights, no one would mistake the quintessentially racist character of such a state.

Israel is an apartheid state, founded on pillage and predicated on exclusivity. Rights flow from ethnic and religious identity.

How is this to end?

There are over five million settlers of European origin in South Africa. The Afrikaaner population and those of British descent have lived in South Africa for many generations. Yet, very few people, let alone those purporting to be advocates of self-determination for Blacks in South Africa, propose two states — a European white state with guaranteed security abutting a demilitarized, subordinate African state.

A dependent Bantustan alongside an apartheid state is a mockery of self-determination — whether in South Africa, colonial Rhodesia and Algeria — or apartheid Israel.

In Israel, no less than in South Africa, minimum justice requires dismantling the apartheid state and replacing it with a democratic secular Palestine, where Jews and Arabs, Christians and Moslems, live together with equal rights and opportunities.

Apartheid Israel cannot exist without the U.S. treasury. Since 1948, $92 billion of U.S. tax money — $6 billion in 1987 alone — have financed Israel, a state built on expulsion, dispossession and subjugation. The American people have no interest in subsidizing the world's fourth largest military power or the torment of the Palestinian people. **End all aid now!**

The response to four decades of outrageous tyranny exists — in the stone throwing children of Jabaliya, the Beach Camp, Balata and Dheisheh. It is echoed in those Israeli Jews who resist the oppression of others.

Theirs is the struggle, slingshots in hand, of David against Goliath.

Theirs is the passion for a life without oppression.

Theirs is the vision of a country shorn of racist dominion.

Palestinians and Jews, free at last from discrimination and injustice, will forge lasting peace only in a democratic and secular society where elementary rights are accorded to all.

Extend your hand to the heroic people of Palestine.

Support the campaign to end all aid to apartheid Israel.

Join the worldwide call for a democratic and secular Palestine.

U.S. SIGNERS:

Samir Abed-Rabbo, publisher, Amana Press; **Philip Agee**; **Bashar Al-Asadi**; **Rashid Al-Banna**; **Dr. Ali Alboosi**; **Robert Allen**, author; **Prof. Abbas Alnasrawi**, U. of Vermont; **Prof. Stanley Anderson**, U.C.S.B.; **Prof. Miguel Angel**, Laney College; **Dr. Philip Antypas**; **Joe W. Aossey**; **Prof. Halem Baraket**, Georgetown Univ.; **George Barghought**, Arab Amer. Assn.; **Prof. Sam Beck**, Assoc. Dean, New School for Soc. Res.; **Prof. Martin Bendersky**, Rider College; **Mary Benns**, Co-chair, Gtr. Balt. Rainbow Coal.; **Rabbi Elmer Berger**; **Ronald Bleier**, Educ. for Soc. Responsib.; **Prof. Carl Boggs**, U.S.C.; **Kamal J. Boullata**, artist; **Kay Boyle**; **Elombe Brath**, Chair, Patrice Lumumba Coal.; **Lenni Brenner**, author; **Kye Briesath**; **Bob Brown**, Balt. Ctte. in Solid. with the Palestinian People; **Elaine Brown**; **Alexander Buchman**; **Cynthia Burke**, Pres., Transp. Communic. Union, 1310, Minn.; **Rena Cacoullos**, Young Socialist Alliance; **David W. Campbell**, Chevron Unit Chair, O.C.A.W. 1-547; **Nick Castle**, film director; **Shirley Ceresesto**, Prof. Emer., Cal. State Long Beach; **Mary Chamelly**, Palestine Solid. Ctte., Chi.; **Lynn Chandler**, songwriter; **Carole Courey**; **Michael Cowan**, Exec. Dir., Natl. Lawyers Guild; **Tom Culotta**, Pres., Cmmty. Survival Ctr.; **Prof. Shawkat J. Dallal**, Utica College; **Prof. Mike Davis**, U.C.L.A.; **Rev. Robert N. Davis**, Grace Episcopal Church, Utica; **Prof. William Doyle**, L.A. Southwest College; **Gerald Dunbar**, atty.; **Prof. Clifford DuRand**, Morgan State Univ.; **Prof. John Edmond**, M.I.T.; **Fouzi El-Asmar**, author; **Prof. Hassan El-Nouty**, U.C.L.A.; **Lawrence Ferlinghetti**; **Prof. Robert A. Fernia**, Univ. of Texas; **Carl Finamore**; **James Marston Fitch**, Prof. Emer., Columbia Univ.; **Prof. Carolyn Fleuhr Lobban**, R. I. College; **Donald Freed**, playwright; **Prof. Nancy Gallagher**, U.C.S.B.; **Prof. Mario T. Garcia**, Chair, Chicano Studies Dept., U.C.S.B.; **Kathleen Geathers**, Coord., N.E. Ohio Anti-Apartheid Ctte.; **Jack Geiger**, CUNY Physicians for Human Rights; **John George**, Supervisor, Alameda Cnty., Calif.; **Suhair Ghanim**; **Janet Gibson**, Alameda Peace Educ. Net.; **Earl Gilman**, Net. of Solid. with Chile; **Jim Guyette**, former Pres., Local P-9, Austin, Minn.; **Jerry Hall**, Pres., SEIU 535, L.A.; **Dr. Muhammad Hallaj**, Ed., *Palestine Perspectives*; **Nathan Hare**, psychologist; **Prof. Bryce Harris**, Occidental College; **James Haughton**, Dir., Harlem Fight Back; **Brian Heron**, Celtic Art Ctr.; **Dr. Will**

L. Herzfeld, Pastor, Bethlehem Lutheran Church; **Carrie Hewitt**, Exec. Bd., AFSCME 3357; **Richard Hill**, C. Amer. Solid. Ctte.; **Prof. Patricia Hills**, art historian; **Rod Holt**; **Prof. Ruth Hubbard**, Harvard Univ.; **Clyde Johnson**, Pres., Black Employees Assn., L. A.; **Dr. Hymon T. Johnson**, U.C.S.B.; **Prof. Theophile Karam**, Cypress College; **Mujid Kazimi**, Dir., Fin. Aid, M.I.T.; **Fathi Khalil**, atty.; **Prof. Baheej Khleif**, Worcester State College; **Morris Kight**, Gay & Lesbian Concerns; **Janet Koenig**, artist; **Tamara Kohns**; **Ron Kovic**, peace activist; **Seymour Kramer**, Steward, U.T.U. 1741; **William M. Kuntsler**, atty.; **Felix S. Kury**, instructor, S.F. State Univ.; **Catherine R. Kusic Koppel**, Coord., Nicaragua Info. Ctr., Calif.; **Prof. Robert M. Laffey**, R. I. College; **Edwin L. Laing**, atty.; **Mark Lane**, atty; **P.J. Laska**, poet; **Hannah Lessinger**, journalist, *The Guardian*; **Bill Leumer**, Pres., I.A.M. 565; **Bridie Letzer**, Irish activist; **Dr. Alfred M. Lilienthal**, author; **Prof. Sheldon B. Liss**, U. of Akron; **Prof. Richard Lobban**, R. I. College; **Prof. Froben Lozada**, Merritt College; **Chokwe Lumumba**, Natl. Conf. of Black Lawyers; **Gretchen Mackler**, State Council, Calif. Teachers Assn.; **Jeff Mackler**; **Victor Marchetti**, Ed., *New American Perspectives*; **Bill May**, atty.; **Prof. Jesse McDade**, Morgan State Univ.; **Ralph McGehee**, author, "Deadly Deceits"; **Ann E. Menasche**, atty.; **Jessica Mitford**; **Abbas Mohammed**, Palestine Solid. Ctte.; **Dr. William Monsour**; **Lucetta Mowry**, Prof. Emer., Wellesley College; **Prof. Carlos Muñoz, Jr.**, U.C. Berkeley; **Prof. Kamal Naffa**, Fullerton College; **Muhammad Najab**; **Ken Nash**; **Rev. Howard Nash**, St. John's United Methodist Church; **Kweilin Nassar**, Steering Ctte., Gtr. Pitts. A.D.C.; **Prof. J.B. Neilands**, U.C. Berkeley; **Pat Norman**, Co-chair, 1987 March on Washington for Lesbian & Gay Rights; **George Novack**, author; **Richard Ochs**, Balt. Emer. Response Net.; **Earl Ofari**, Black author; **Prof. Richard Ohmann**, Wesleyan Univ.; **Prof. Bertell Ollman**, N.Y.U.; **Walter Oszkowski**; **Palestinian Cultural Club, U.S.C.**; **Prof. Kostis Papadontanakis**, Essex Cmmty. College; **Prof. Michael Parenti**, political scientist; **Dr. Linus Pauling**, Nobel Laureate - Chemistry, Peace; **Prof. Fred Pfeil**, Wesleyan Univ.; **Prof. Gerard Pigeon**, Chair, Black Studies Dept., U.C.S.B.; **Christopher E. Platten**, atty.; **Daniel Plattner**, Johns Hopkins Univ. Coal. for a Free S. Africa; **Marilyn Plumlee**; **Leonard Potash**, Rep., AFSCME Council 57, L.A.; **Martha Quinn**, Chair, Evanston Ctte. on C. Amer.; **Prof. Peter Rachleff**, Macalester College; **William Randolph**, All African Peoples Rev. Party; **Richard O. Recknagel**, Prof. Emer., Case Western Reserve Univ.; **Prof. Roddey Reid**, Middlebury College; **Richard Reilly**, Mid-West Reg. Coord., Palestine Solid. Ctte; **Wilson Riles, Jr.**, Oakland City Council; **Prof. Ann Robertson**, S.F. State Univ.; **Prof. Stewart Robinson**, Cleve. State Univ.; **Tony Rodriguez**, atty., Palestine 8; **Walter Rosenblum**, Prof. Emer., Brooklyn College; **Trudy Rudnick**, Sec., AFT 3882; **John Russo**, Dir., Labor Studies, Youngstown State Univ.; **Tony Russo**, Pentagon Papers defendant; **The Very Rev. Hanna S. Sakkab**, Arch. Priest, Orthodox Church, Syracuse; **Prof. Najib Saliba**, Worcester State College; **Ann Salmeron**, member, Boston CASA; **George Saunders**, translator; **Ralph**

Schoenman, Exec. Dir., Campaign to End All Aid to Israel; **Theodore Schoenman**, author; **Fridtjof Schroder**, Prof. Emer., CCNY; **Stephen Schumacher**, Dir., Ctr. for Peace Ed., Cinn.; **Prof. James Scully**, U. of Conn.; **Amin Shafie**, U. of Cinn.; **Muhjah Shakir**; **Bassam Shalhoub**; **Prof. Steven Shaviro**, U. of Wash.; **Roland Sheppard**, Delegate, S.F. Labor Council; **Mya Shone**; **Mustafa Siam**, Chair, United American-Arab Congress; **Paul N. Siegel**, Prof. Emer., L.I.U.; **Art Slater**, Issues Chair, Rainbow Coal., Cinn.; **Loretta Smith**, filmmaker; **Prof. Neil Smith**, Rutgers Univ.; **Rev. Donald L. Smith**, Synod of Sthrn. Calif. & Hawaii; **Jan Snipper**, East Bay CLUW; **Martha Stephens**, Ed., *Cinn. Review of Politics & Art*; **Prof. Jim Syfers**, S.F. State Univ.; **Harryet Tara**, journalist; **Rutthy Taubb**, songwriter; **Lynn Taylor**, Exec. Bd., AFSCME 1930; **Mary Jane Thacker**, Dir., Christ. Educ., United Methodist Church, San Jose; **Prof. Carol Thompson**, U.S.C.; **Daniel Thompson**, poet; **John Trinkl**, *The Guardian*; **Kwame Touré**, formerly Stokely Carmichael; **Valerie Van Isler**; **Rev. David Van Strien**, Chair, Unitarian Universalists for Justice in the Mid. East, Peterboro, N.H.; **Gore Vidal**; **Kurt Vonnegut**; **David Wald**; **Alice Walker**, writer, poet; **Sister Miriam Ward**, Trinity College, Vt.; **Roger Wareham**, lecturer, Ctr. for Law & Soc. Justice, CUNY; **James Mac Warren**, Socialist Workers Party; **Prof. Gloria Watkins**, Yale Univ.; **Nat Weinstein**, Natl. Sec., Socialist Action; **Suzi Weissman**, KPFK, L. A.; **Prof. Kevin Whitfield**, U. of Mass.; **Ron Wilkins**, Unity in Action; **Prof. Gretchen Willging**, Essex Cmmty. College; **John T. Williams**, Former Pres., Teamsters 208, L.A.; **Robert F. Williams**, Monroe Civil Rights Defendant; **Louis Wolf**; **Dr. Tony Wolf**, Rev., Presbyterian Church, Irvine, Calif.; **Claudia Wright**, journalist; **Dr. Munir Zaitoon**; **Raouf Zarrouk**, art historian; **Faith Zeadey**, Pres., Arab-American Univ. Graduates; **John J. Zogby**, Americans for Mid. East Peace.

INTERNATIONAL SIGNERS:

ALGERIA: Brajin Boukhaj, MDA; **BELGIUM: Prof. J. Gadisseur**, U. of Liege; **Julien Gallemi**, Pres., F.N. Hertal Labor Fed.; **Paul Gruselin**, Ed., *La Walonie*; **Prof. Jamoulle**, ULG Liege; **Prof. Y. Lion**, U. of Liege; **P. Longe**, Res. Dir., FNRS; **Jean Claude Renda**, journalist, RPTB; **Jacques Yerna**, Gen. Sec., FGTB, Liege-Huiy-Waremme; **BRAZIL: Regis De Castro Andrade**, Dir. of Res., Ctr. for Contemporary Cultural Studies; **Raymundo Faoro**, historian; **Florestan Fernandez**, Natl. Deputy; **Prof. Paolo Freire**, author, "Pedagogy of the Oppressed"; **Dr. Anna Volochko**, Dir., Cmmty. Med., Sao Paolo; **Prof. Francisco Weffort**, Sao Paolo Univ.; **CANADA: Father Shafiq Farah**; **Najib Farah**, Info. Dir., Palestinian Assn; **Mohammed Ghieh**, V.P., Quebec Palestine Assn.; **Prof. James A. Graff**, U. of Toronto; Pres., Near East Cult. & Educ. Fdtn. of Canada; **Bohdan Krawchenko**, Dir., Can. Inst. of Ukranian Stud., U. of Alberta; **Prof. Pierre Lacasse**, Pres. Quebec Palestine Assn.; **Barry Weis-**

leder, Pres., Ontario Pub. Ser. Employees Union 595; **FRANCE: Jean Pierre Barrois**, linguist; **Maître Delphine Bouit**, atty.; **Pierre Broué**, Dir., Leon Trotsky Instit.; **Maître Capelle-Hallier**, atty.; **Maître Gilbert Collard**, atty.; **Prof. François Guérin; Georges Grandin**, Dir., Geology Ctr., Ecole des Mines ; **Prof. Paul Milliez**, Hon. Dean, Broussais Med. School; **Richard Nijoule**, mathematician; **Maître Perralta-Lequerré**, atty.; **Maurice Rajfus**, journalist; **Maître Helene Rubinstein-Carrera**, atty.; **Daniel Seldjouk**, journalist; **Michel Vale**, translator; **GREECE: Costas Bakirdis**, Gen. Sec., Fed. of Indust. Workers, CGT; **Franceskos Faturos**, Gen. Sec., Athens Labor Council; **Mikalis Karalambidis**, Central Ctte., PASOK; **Vangelis Konstaninou**, V.P., Fed. of Indust. Workers, CGT; **Dionisis Mouzakis**, V.P., Elect. Workers Fed.; **Georgus Zerbas**, Gen. Sec., Salonica Labor Council; **GREAT BRITAIN: Jim Boumelha**, Exec. Ctte., Natl. Union of Journalists; **Ken Cameron**, Gen. Sec., Firebrigade Union; **Tamara Deutscher; Jake Eccleston**, Dep. Gen. Sec., Natl. Union of Journalists; **Dr. Donald A. Filtzer**, Sr. Res. Fellow, U. of Birmingham; **Baruch Hirson**, historian; **Quintin Hoare**, author; **Veronica Marris**, Namibia Support Ctte.; **Nadim Shehadi**, Oxford Univ.; **Hillel Ticktin**, Ed., *Critique*; lecturer, U. of Glasgow; **Ros Young**, Namibia Support Ctte.; **N. IRELAND: Gerry Adams**, M.P., Pres., Sinn Fein; **Bernadette Devlin McAliskey**; **ISRAEL: Merav Devir**, Ctte. for the Freedom of Expression of Palestinians and Israelis; **Abraham Heilbronn**, psychologist; **Akiva Orr**, author; **Osnat Ron**, "RETURN"; **Shimon Tzabar**, playwright; **World Org. of Jews from Islamic Countries** (not WOJAC); **A.H. Yahooram**, Gen. Sec., World Org. of Jews from Islamic Countries; **MEXICO: Adolfo Gilly**, author; **NORWAY: Dr. Steinar Berge; Grette Klotrupp Larsen; Dr. Troy Rusli**, Prof., Red Cross Hospital, Oslo; **PERU: Senator Rolando Breña Pantoja; Prof. Humberto Campodonico Sanchez**, U. of San Marcos; **Senator Javier Diez-Canseco; Senator Genaro Ledesma**, Pres., FOCEP; **Senator Andrés Luna Vargas; Moises Palomino**, Pres., Natl. Miners and Metalworkers Fed.; **Enrique Rodriguez**, Gen. Sec., Natl. Teachers Fed.; **Juan Rojas Vargas**, Gen. Sec., Peruvian Peasants Fed.; **Carlos Salazar Pasache**, Intl. Rel., Peruvian Educ. Workers Union; **Yeude Simon**, Natl. Deputy, Co-Pres., ANP; **Leonor Zamora**, Workers Party; **SPAIN: Juan Francisco Anton Rodriguez**, Pres., Assn. of Young Doctors, Alicante; **Frances Casares**, Deputy, Catalonian Parliament; **Faustino Cordon**, biologist; **Juan Jose Diaz Sanchez**, CNT, Valencia; **Justo Fernandez**, Gen. Sec., Bank Workers Fed., UGT; **Regina Fuente**, Pres., Assn. of Young Lawyers, Valencia; **Julia Garcia**, Exec. Bd., Madrid Neighbor. Assn.; **Marianne Hermitte**, film producer; **Gregorio Lopez Raymundo**, ex-Pres., P.S.U.C.; **Francisco Manuel**, atty.; **Peré Mayor**, Deputy, Valencia; **Blas Ortega**, Pres., Assn. of Young Doctors, Valencia; **Jose Antonio Pallin**, Pres., Natl. Human Rights Assn.; **Ionis Peñaroja Gonzalez**, Pres., Assn. of Young Doctors, Castellon; **Prof. Vicent Pitarch**, Exec. Bd., Unitat del Poble, Valencia; **Roberto Ruiz**, Fin. Sec., Health Workers Fed., CCOO, Valencia; **Manuel San Nicolas**, Gen. Sec., Bank Workers Fed., UGT, Catalonia; **Joaquin Sicilia**, La Crida;

Jaume Soler, Mayor of Arbucias, leader of La Crida; **Ramon Terrades**, Pres., Metalworkers Ctte., UGT, Catalonia; **Prof. Pedro Vilanova**, U. of Barcelona; **SWITZERLAND: Eric Decarro**, Pres., Fed. of Trade Unions, Geneva; **Erica Deuber-Pauli**, Deputy, Geneva; **Dr. Nago Humbert**; **Armand Magnin**, Deputy, Geneva; **Berthier Perregaux**, Deputy, Geneva; **Jean Spielmann**, Federal Deputy; **Jean Ziegler**, Federal Deputy; **VENEZUELA: Moises Moleiro**, Natl. Deputy.

[For more information on the Campaign to End All Aid to Israel/For a Democratic Secular Palestine, contact: P.O. Box 90609, Santa Barbara, CA 93190-0609.]

Available from Veritas Press

- *Prisoners of Israel* by Mya Shone and Ralph Schoenman, $12.95

Forthcoming Titles

- *Homage to Palestine: A Critical History* by Ralph Schoenman
- *Against the Crime of Silence: Proceedings of the International Tribunal on United States War Crimes in Indochina* (Expanded Edition: "20 Years Later")
- *1905* by Leon Trotsky
- *Peasant Struggles in India* by A.R. Desai
- *John Brown's Bodies: A Participant's Account*
- *Woman, Not Inferior to Man, Early 18th Century Feminist Essays* by "Sophia," a person of quality

Translations by Theodore Schoenman & Helen Benedek Schoenman:

- *The Dogs of Paul Szontagh and Other Stories* by Kálmán Mikszáth
- *Folk Tales From Old Hungary: The George Gaal Collection*
- *Travels in North America* by Agoston Haraszthy
- *Angi Vera and Other Novellas* by Endre Vészi
- *Crying Dolls and Other Children's Stories* by J. Tersánszky

About the Author

Ralph Schoenman was Executive Director of the Bertrand Russell Peace Foundation, in which capacity he conducted negotiations with numerous heads of state. He secured the release of political prisoners in many countries and initiated the International Tribunal on U.S. War Crimes in Indo-China, of which he was Secretary General.

Long active in political life, he initiated the Committee of 100 which organized mass civil disobedience against nuclear weapons and U.S. bases in Great Britain. He was founder and Director of the Vietnam Solidarity Campaign and Director of the Who Killed Kennedy Committee.

He has also been a leader of the Committee for Artistic and Intellectual Freedom in Iran and Co-Director of the Committee in Defense of the Palestinian and Lebanese Peoples and of American Workers and Artists for Solidarity.

He is currently Executive Director of the Palestine Campaign which calls for an end to all aid to Israel and for a democratic and secular Palestine.

His previous books include "Bertrand Russell: Philosopher of the Century," "Death and Pillage in the Congo: A Study of Western Rule," which he co-authored with Khalid Ahmed Zaki and "Prisoners of Israel" written with Mya Shone.